Letter from the Editors

Wow! That's all we can say. Thank you to everyone who has helped make the *Anglotopia Magazine* such a success from its first issue. It was so popular, we didn't order enough from the printer and it sold out! We did not anticipate that. And you can be sure we'll be ordering plenty of extras for this issue. Subscribing to the *Anglotopia Magazine* isn't just about getting a great lineup of articles, it's about supporting a global community of passionate Anglophiles and with the success of the magazine, the future of Anglotopia is safe.

The magazine has changed Anglotopia for the better. It has allowed us to invest in longer form writing that just wouldn't work on the website. This month we have two fantastic features - a tour of an abandoned Tube Station and a chronicle of our day in Oxford last February. We've given these articles room to breathe and inserted tons of great pictures.

The feedback from the magazine has been all positive - people loved the high quality paper, many are keeping the magazine as a keepsake or conversation piece on their coffee tables. People loved the beautiful photography that we were able to license. And most of all, people loved the variety of articles on all things British. This month, the lineup is slightly different based on what worked and what didn't work in the first issue. We hope you enjoy this issue as much as the last one.

Also, a bit of good news. Last month, we wrote about Wentworth Woodhouse and how it was under threat and in need of restoration. The day after we went to press, news broke that the house has been sold to SAVE Britain's Heritage and will be restored under a multi-year plan as well as opened to the public under the auspices of the National Trust. We're so pleased that one of Britain's most beautiful stately homes has been saved for the nation. We hope to see it ourselves one day.

Cheers,
Jonathan & Jackie Thomas
Editors and Publishers
Anglotopia

Cover: Radcliffe Camera, Oxford, Back Cover: Spring Flowers, Burford, Inside Back Cover: Burford, Oxfordshire

Table of Contents

About the Magazine

The Anglotopia Magazine is published by Anglotopia LLC, a USA registered Corporation. All contents copyrighted. Letters to the Editors may be addressed to:

Anglotopia LLC
1101 Cumberland Xing
Valparaiso, IN 46383 U

Corrections

In *Names of London* we incorrectly stated that Londe was the Italian name for London. It is actually Londra. Also, in many European language the r is not silent in Londres.

Also in *Names of London* it was the Greater London Council that was abolished in 1986. The London County Council existed before then and was abolished in 1965 when the GLC was founded.

In the *Manchester* article we mentioned the Coronation Street set tour being a good thing to do - unfortunately, this attraction closed last year.

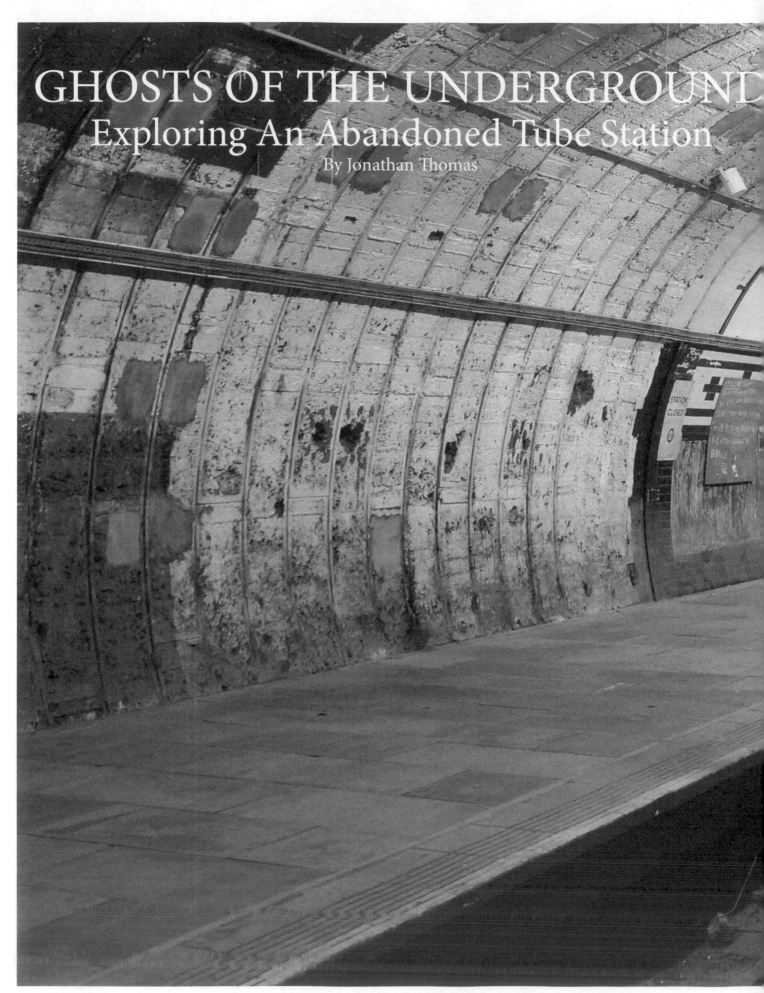

GHOSTS OF THE UNDERGROUND
Exploring An Abandoned Tube Station
By Jonathan Thomas

One of the entrances to Aldwych Station

It's hard to imagine that in this modern day and age that there would be anywhere in London that's abandoned, forgotten, and out of use. Until very recently London was home to the most expensive real estate on the planet. But yet there are pockets of London that are abandoned. The London Underground is home to several abandoned Tube Stations. These so-called 'ghost stations' went out of service for many different reasons but there are several of them and occasionally they're opened up for tours for curious Londonphiles to explore.

Hidden London is a program run by the London Transport Museum that provides the opportunity for enthusiasts to explore the old or abandoned parts of the Tube network that are no longer in use. One would think that something like this would be a bit of a niche interest but whenever they offer tickets for these tours, they sell out within minutes. It's something I've personally always wanted to do. There's a certain romance about abandoned Tube stations, forgotten to history, covered in the dust of Londoners past and present. It's no surprise that many of these are used as ad hoc shooting locations for TV shows and films.

When a new round of Hidden London tours was announced last fall, I prepared for disappointment, I always managed to miss out on getting tickets. I keep an eye on these things since I am a Tube enthusiast. I knew what time they were being released, and I knew to be at the computer ready to buy. My goal was to tour Down Street station, famous as being a bunker during World War II for Churchill's wartime government. Sadly, it was sold out before my fingers could move fast enough. I tried the second station on offer and was similarly locked out. I clicked into the third option for tours of Aldwych Station and with luck it was not sold out - in fact there were plenty of options available in February 2016 (about five months from when I was booking). I immediately booked a ticket for the tour and couldn't believe my luck.

Then it hit me, I just bought tickets to a tour that would require me to book an entire trip to Britain from the USA. I take my interest in the Tube very seriously. The months passed and I booked a trip to London using my hard-earned airline miles. And on Saturday, February 20, I found myself standing in a queue outside Aldwych Abandoned Tube station

One of the main disused passenger tunnels below the ground

waiting to get inside. It was all very surreal and exciting.

The first question probably running through your head is why would they ever close a Tube station? The story of Aldwych is not typical of the Underground. When the various Tube lines were built, they were built by competing companies (with a profit motive). Aldwych was opened in 1907 with the name Strand, after the street on which it is located, and was the terminus of the short Piccadilly line branch from Holborn that was a relic of the merger of two railway schemes. Over the years, there were many plans to make the station a through station to connect it to the rest of the network, but it remained a dead end of sorts for the Piccadilly line and due to low passenger volume, it was eventually closed in 1994 (the elevators needed to be replaced and the cost of doing so exceeded the profits generated by passengers using the station). The guides joked that the station was now making more money than it ever did doing semi-regular tours.

Our tour began in the entry hallways where the staff explained the history of the station and why it was closed. The guides were a fountain of knowledge on the various decorations and architectural styles. The style of the station very much matches the styles of other Piccadilly line stations. The entry way features lovely green tiles, and over the years the station has also been a testing ground for designs used in future stations.

There were about 20 fellow Tube enthusiasts on the tour - all with high powered cameras clicking and clacking away. It was such a rare treat to be able to explore the station that there was an air of excitement. It was one of many tours that day, yet the staff never appeared bored or annoyed at all the tourists wanting to poke around their station.

After introductory remarks, it was time to descend to the out of service platforms. Since the Victorian elevators no longer worked, visitors were required to descend 160 or so steps to the platforms. This wasn't so bad going down and it went by quite quickly. Going back up when the tour was over was quite exhausting, and I felt quite sorry for the heavily pregnant woman in front of me who had to climb back up!

The most interesting aspect of the station's history was its use as a bomb shelter during both World

Down the stairs to the platform level

The elevator lobby at platform level

One of the out-of-service platforms (it's been blocked off)

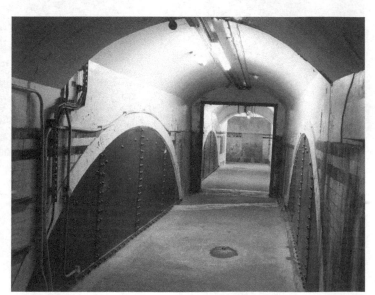
The bridge between the platforms

Architectural detail on tunnel structure

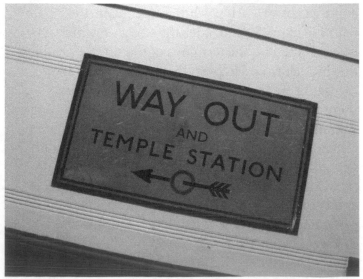
Exit sign

War I and World War II. Many people don't realize that the Blitz in World War II was not the first time that Londoners had to shelter from German bombs. World War I also featured several great Zeppelin raids that inflicted mass damage on London. Aldwych proved useful as a shelter not once, but twice (and let's hope never again).

During World War II, one of the disused platforms was used to store art from the National Gallery. It's rather an interesting thought to think of the nation's Turners and Constables chilling out on a disused Tube platform. It turns out, though, that the damp station wasn't the best place to store valuable paintings, so they shifted to the storage of statues and other works of art that wouldn't be damaged by water (looking up you can see the calcite deposits leaking from the ceiling - art doesn't like that!)

The most famous tenants during World War II were the Elgin Marbles from the British Museum. The Marbles were originally from the Parthenon in Greece and Britain's possession of them is controversial. Despite this, Britain has cared for them well and stored them for protection when needed. The guides told us how they had to be winched down with a crane through the elevator shaft. When they were removed after the war, they decided this was too dangerous to repeat so they took them out by train to a neighbouring station where they could be more easily removed. The other platforms were used to house people sheltering from bombs during the London Blitz (which took place at the end of 1940) and the V1 and V2 raids later in the war.

I was most interested in the station's use as a shelter during World War II. The station was not particularly deep, so the residents of the shelter would still have had the terrifying experience of hearing bombs dropping all around them as it was in the center of London. Conditions for those in the shelter were not great - people would have to queue for hours for a place and sometimes they did not get them. Racks of beds were provided for people to sleep, the platforms were closed so hammocks were strung across the tracks. Facilities were very basic at first - a bucket sufficed as a toilet at the beginning (though this changed later on).

The British with their Blitz spirit would make the most of the situation, children would play together. Sometimes concerts were held from the station and broadcast to the rest of the country as a propaganda

Key Facts

- Station went into operation in 1907
- Station closed in 1994
- Station renamed Aldwych from Strand in 1915
- Dead end on the Piccadilly Line
- Used by only 400 passengers a day
- Used often in film and TV Movies such as "V for Vendetta", "James Bond", "Mr Selfridge" and more.
- Open at select times for tours. Contact the London Transport Museum for details.

move to show that Britain was not afraid. Simply acting like nothing was amiss was crucial to maintain good morale as Britain faced its most existential threat.

At one point during the war, more than 100,000 people were sheltering in Tube stations all over the network. At first the British government did not want people to do this - but as there were no adequate deep level bomb shelters, they relented and began to allow the stations to be used as long as it didn't interfere with London's wartime transport needs.

While the facilities were basic at the beginning, by 1941 there was a first aid post, proper latrines (instead of the bucket), a canteen that wasn't subject to rationing, (which meant all the hot yummy food you could eat) a library, and other entertainments. It was all about making a home away from home to make the situation bearable.

Londoners made the best of their time in the shelter - there was plenty to do when you weren't sleeping, though that's what most people did (in between copious amounts of tea). As the war progressed and the Blitz officially ended, use of the station as a shelter tapered off. It went up again during the V1 and V2 raids in the latter part of the war. The public shelter closed when the war ended in May 1945.

As the station is in a disused condition, it is very much like it was in the 1940s as the station has not had updates familiar to later Tube stations. This gives you a unique look at how life would have been like during its use as a bomb shelter during the wars.

Old advertisements and movie poster props (the 'Station Closed' posters are from a movie)

The other platform, still connected to the Tube network, with disused train parked

The tour was good enough to highlight this and even had recordings of people who remembered their experiences sheltering in the Tube.

After the war, passenger service was not restored until 1946. And even then, passenger numbers were very low - it was never a widely used station because not many people lived in the neighborhood it served. There were no major tourist attractions nearby and many workers used other Tube stations (some of which were quicker to walk to than to take a train to). So after the war the station became a testing bed for future Tube station designs (examples of which you can see on the tour).

Since the station was essentially a dead end on the Piccadilly line, it was not widely used when it was re-opened. It was kept open for convenience sake, but by the early 1990s, it was clear that keeping the station open was a waste of public money. So, the station was locked up and the passengers were told to go to neighboring stations. Since the station was closed it has had a second life as a shooting location for film and TV.

If you're a fan of British TV and film, this station will look very familiar to you. Whenever a TV show or film crew needs a Tube station, they'll usually hire Aldwych. There's even a full-scale Tube train gathering dust at one of the platforms suitable for filming use. What films have used the station? "Atonement", "V for Vendetta", "28 Weeks Later", and "The Imitation Game" amongst others were filmed in the station. There are artifacts from the filming all around the station (there are many posters and advertisements that don't belong there but were left by careless film crews). The hit TV shows "Sherlock" and "Mr Selfridge" have also made use of the station many times. The station is also used as a training facility for the Tube's emergency services.

You get a rather eerie feeling walking through the silent and dimly lit corridors of the disused station. You can feel the ghosts of London's past as you explore the empty station. There's a very lovely smell - a combination of grime and dust that could only be in a place that was touched by many layers of peoples lives through history. It's a terrifying prospect to imagine being sheltered there during World War II and it makes one grateful that such a thing is not necessary anymore.

Overall, I was very pleased with the Hidden London tour. The staff were friendly, knowledgeable, and a bit funny as well. The London Transport

Other Abandoned Stations

- **British Museum** - Opened in 1909 but it was never widely used and closed in 1933 - though would be useful today!
- **Trafalgar Square** - Closed in the 1970s when traffic was diverted to the new Charing Cross Station.
- **Charing Cross** - The Jubilee Platforms themselves were closed in 1999 as they were bypassed.
- **Tower of London** - Shortest life of a Tube station - opened in 1882 and closed in 1884. Tower Hill replaced it.
- **Uxbridge Road** - One of the oldest stations on the network - it was opened in 1869 but was bombed during World War II and never re-opened.
- **York Road** - Opened in 1906 and used sporadically until 1932 when it was closed due to low passenger numbers.
- **Down Street** - Opened in 1907 and closed in 1932 because snobby Mayfair residents didn't use the Tube. It later found a second life as a shelter during World War II for Churchill's War Cabinet (this one is also open to tours).
- **St. Mary's** - The street level building was destroyed by a bomb during World War II, but the underground structures remain closed and abandoned.
- **Heathrow Terminal 5** - Platforms built ahead of time when Terminal 5 was in the planning stages. They were built in the wrong location and never used.

Museum will continue to run Hidden London tours throughout the year. It's best to sign up on its website to find out when the tours will be. I definitely want to try and explore some of the other disused stations, such as the one at Down Street where Churchill's government holed up during German air raids. There's also a deep level shelter in Clapham open occasionally that was used during the war and also for refugees after the war. The guides assured us that Aldwych would be on future tours so you can have the same opportunity to explore London's history like I did.

Great British Houses
St. Michael's Mount

St Michael's Mount, a stunning former medieval monastery and sprawling castle that is set atop an offshore island and is only accessible on foot during low tide, seems very much like the setting of a fairy tale. But the tumultuous Middle Ages, Henry VIII's dissolution of the monasteries and more contemporary British crises such as World War II have made St Michael's Mount an important historical stronghold, scenic but strategic. Today, St Michael's Mount offers visitors a picturesque castle, well preserved but also much altered over the centuries, and elegant sub-tropical gardens with a pretty harbour below.

There is evidence that St Michael's Mount was inhabited at least as early as the Neolithic era (circa 4000-2500 BCE) and it may have been used as a trade port for continental tradesmen picking up Cornish tin bound for the Mediterranean during the first few centuries AD. Whether the Mount was the ancient port known as Ictis is unclear, but what we do know for certain is that Edward the Confessor gave the Mount to the Norman abbey of Mont Saint-Michel in 1135. Benedictine monks from this abbey were invited to establish a priory in Cornwall, an invitation they accepted, and over the next few centuries, carefully and painstakingly built their church.

In 1425, the monks also laid a rough causeway that, at ebb tide, makes the mount accessible on foot from the landward side. The monks lived in peace for a number of years until St Michael's Mount became a strategic base for Perkin Warbeck, a pretender to the throne of King Henry VII. After Warbeck's failed rebellion during the War of the

The island on a postcard from 1900

Key Facts

- St Michael's Mount is a small island, monastery and castle located in Mount's Bay, [in Marazion] Cornwall, England.
- A priory was first built on the site in 1135 and the castle and surrounding buildings were built over the succeeding seven centuries.
- The Mount passed through many owners before Colonel St Aubyn bought it in 1659. His descendants owned the mount until year 1954 when it was given to the National Trust. The family still live there.

Roses, he sought refuge in St Michael's Mount with his notoriously beautiful wife Catherine, one of many women who thought they had married a king during these tumultuous times but who never did become queen.

Following King Henry VIII's Dissolution of the Monasteries (1536-1540), St Michael's Mount was occupied by a number of crown-approved military governors who kept the fortified island in good shape and defended it against Parliamentarian forces who tried to take it in 1642. Their victory was short-lived as St Michael's Mount was surrendered to Parliamentarian forces in 1646 and fell under the command of John St Aubyn, a Parliamentary colonel who was nominated governor and began to adapt the existing building on the mount, part monastery, part castle, into a residence. Descendants of John St Aubyn, the Lords St Levan, live at St Michael's Mount to this day and are responsible for the many architectural transformations the building has undergone.

Some parts of the medieval incarnation of St Michael's Mount remain such as the gatehouse, the converted Lady Chapel, and the church and refectory with garrison quarters underneath. The church is thought to date back to the 13th century and St Michael's chapel to the 15th. What was initially the monastic refectory, built in the 12th century, became the Tudor Great Hall and features a magnificent arch-braced roof. This roof was restored in the 19th century, at which point the room entered the third stage of its existence and became known as the Chevy Chase Room. This name comes from the incredible plaster friezes of hunting scenes that

The Imposing Castle Walls

line its walls. A Jacobean oak table with a full set of monastic chairs completes the imposing effect.

The most revered room at St Michael's Mount is the old monastic Lady Chapel that was gloriously converted into a drawing room during the mid-18th century. With views from the north terrace of the very summit of the island, this carefully conserved Georgian treat has interiors in the style of Strawberry Hill Gothic, featuring pretty pale blue and white ornamentation and a significant landscape of the mount itself by artist John Opie.

The rest of the castle displays the old barracks and museum rooms. A number of other buildings can be found dotted around the castle including a row of late 19th century houses known as Elizabeth Terrace, some of which are occupied by castle employees. You will also find the former stables, laundry, steward's house and two former inns.

What Makes St Michael's Mount Famous?

St Michael's Mount is famous both for historical and mythical reasons. An important Benedictine

priory used as a stronghold by a pretender king, held for the king during the Civil War before being taken by a parliamentarian Colonel, and machine-gunned during World War II, St Michael's Mount has seen its share of real-life warfare. But the mount also has an aura of mystery they has made it the setting of the legend of Jack the Giant Killer and a filming location for various Dracula films. An iconic rocky island on the coast of Cornwall, St Michael's Mount has many stories to tell and is very worth a visit if you're in Cornwall.

Featured in TV and Film

- Dracula (1979)
- Never Say Never Again (1983)
- Johnny English (2003)
- Mariah Mundhi and the Midas Box (2012)

Further Research

- James St Aubyn, A Personal Tour of St Michael's Mount (2010)

The Village on the Island at Low Tide

- McCabe, Helen (1988). Houses and Gardens of Cornwall.

Visiting Information

St Michael's Mount is open to the public, but the opening times are complicated and vary depending on day, month, and season so it is best to visit the website www.stmichaelsmount.co.uk before you visit. When the tide is in, the mount is accessible by one of St Michael's Mount's ferry boats and when it's out, you can walk across the causeway. Entry to both the castle and gardens costs £12.50 per adult and £6.00 per child.

To get to St Michael's Mount by car, travel on the A30 to Penzance then follow the signs for Marazion. There is ample car parking in a seafront car park. You can take the train from London as there is also an intercity train link to Penzance station, from which you can take a local bus or taxi to Marazion. We would recommend renting a car and driving down to Cornwall for the full experience.

Scones! Was there ever a word in the whole of Great Britain to cause such controversy? Is the word said 'sc-oh-nes' or 'sc-o-ns'? What is the best / most correct recipe? With sultanas / raisins / currants or without? And if served with cream, does the jam sit under or over the cream?

The only answers I have for all such predicaments is that what has been done in your family for generations is what should be continued, but don't ask me the answers when marriage unites two people from different traditions. I would suggest that the person who bakes holds the balance of power!

In my family we stick to the 'magic e' producing an 'oh' sound so that the word rhymes with stone.

We follow my grandmother's recipe as we all love dried fruit and we steer clear of the cream question as none of us are particularly keen on it!

For the record, a Devon scone is served with the cream below the jam but a Cornish one has the cream atop the jam.

Jane Colston is the owner of Updown Cottage, a beautiful self-catering cottage located on Gold 'Hovis' Hill in Shaftesbury, Dorset. A beautiful place to stay and enjoy Dorset! http://updowncottage.co.uk

Instructions

- Heat the oven to 220°C, 200°C fan, 425°F, Gas 7 and heat a baking sheet.
- Sift the flour into a large bowl with the baking powder, salt, and sugar.
- Add the butter and with the fingertips only, rub the butter into the flour mixture, very gently, lifting the mixture each time to incorporate air until it looks a bit like breadcrumbs.
- You can also use a food processor but it takes only a minute and sparks a poignant reminder of my mother and grandmother baking every week!
- Mix in the sultanas with a spoon.
- Use a knife to mix the milk and vanilla into the mixture which will be quite sticky.
- Scatter some extra flour onto a clean board or surface and also on to your hands.
- Use a spatula to scrape the scone mixture on to the board then, with your hands, ensure that the mixture is well incorporated but don't knead or over-mix !
- Form the dough into a round shape about 1.5" deep.
- Use a 1.5" circular pastry or cookie cutter to cut out the scones, reforming the dough to make as many as you can.
- Place on to the warmed baking sheet, brush the tops of the scones with the beaten egg and bake for 8-10 minutes until golden.
- Serve slightly warm with butter, clotted cream, jam……. whatever is your choice!
- They also freeze well and can be defrosted and warmed just before serving.

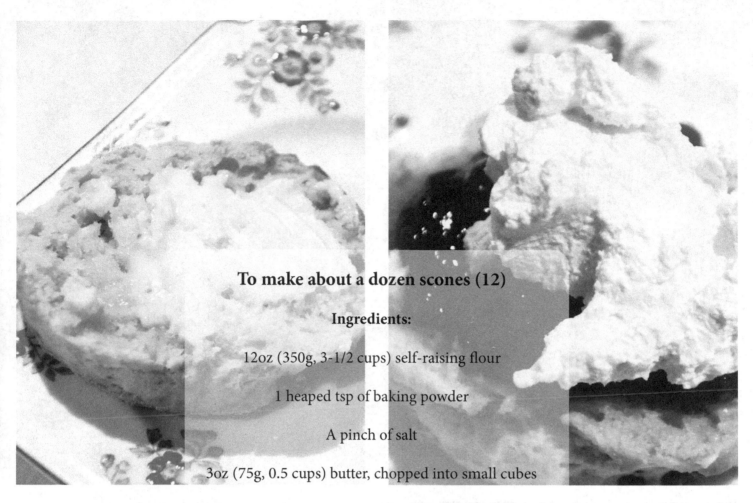

To make about a dozen scones (12)

Ingredients:

12oz (350g, 3-1/2 cups) self-raising flour

1 heaped tsp of baking powder

A pinch of salt

3oz (75g, 0.5 cups) butter, chopped into small cubes

3oz (75g, 1/2 cup) caster sugar

3oz (75g, 1/2 cup) sultanas

1/4pt (175ml, 2/3 cup) milk

1tsp vanilla extract

1 beaten egg for glazing

My scones were photographed on Herbert and Constance's (my grandparents) tea service that they received as a wedding present in 1932 and which I was delighted to inherit.

© Historic England

THEN - LIVERPOOL

This photo was taken in the 1920s as part of one of the first aerial surveys of Britain using the rather new technology of airplanes. At this point in history Liverpool was one of the major centres of shipping for part of the still existent British Empire. This was reflected in the wealth that built the Three Graces, the three buildings at the center of this post. The buildings are: Royal Liver Building, built between 1908-1911 and designed by Walter Aubrey Thomas, Cunard Building, constructed between 1914-1916 and a grade II* listed building and the Port of Liverpool Building, built from 1903-1907 and also grade II* listed. Liverpool was a common disembarkation point for transatlantic liners and also for important trade links with Ireland across the Irish Sea. The confidence of these buildings in their design and architecture are emblematic of how the British felt about their empire and their place at the center of a great empire.

NOW - LIVERPOOL

During World War II, Liverpool was subjected to 80 air raids, which decimated the city. After World War II, Liverpool fell on hard times as the British Empire collapsed in the new post-war, post-imperialist world. Coupled with the containerisation of shipping that made the docks obsolete and the advent of the jet airliners, which reduced the need for transatlantic shipping, Liverpool's economy collapsed. Despite rebuilding efforts, the city still had one of the worst unemployment rates in the Britain. Then a cultural revolution began with a little-known band called The Beatles, who put Liverpool back on the map. In recent years, billions have been invested in city and former docklands, regenerating the local economy to become one of Britain's most beautiful cities. It was the European Capital of Culture in 2008. The Three Graces are still there but they now have other functions and the area around them has been redeveloped into a new arts district with beautiful architecture and new museums. The hope is that Liverpool's brightest days are ahead of it.

LAND OF HOPE AND GLORY

Dear Land of Hope, thy hope is crowned,
God make thee mightier yet!
On Sov'ran brows, beloved, renowned,
Once more thy crown is set.
Thine equal laws, by Freedom gained,
Have ruled thee well and long;
By Freedom gained, by Truth maintained,
Thine Empire shall be strong.

Land of Hope and Glory, Mother of the Free,
How shall we extol thee, who are born of thee?
Wider still and wider shall thy bounds be set;
God, who made thee mighty, make thee mightier yet,
God, who made thee mighty, make thee mightier yet.

Thy fame is ancient as the days,
As Ocean large and wide:
A pride that dares, and heeds not praise,
A stern and silent pride;
Not that false joy that dreams content
With what our sires have won;
The blood a hero sire hath spent
Still nerves a hero son.

By A. C. Benson - 1902

Burford, Oxfordshire During the Diamond Jubilee in 2012

The London Blitz
"London Can Take it"

After a year at war in Europe, Hitler sought to gain the advantage by taking the battle to the doorsteps of the British public. The Luftwaffe began bombing Britain in the hope of terrifying the population into submission and carried on its reign of terror for seven long months. London bore the brunt of Hitler's Blitz, but plucky Londoners kept calm and carried on, and the redoubtable spirit of the Blitz passed into legend.

Key Dates

- 7 September 1940 - First raid of the Blitz
- 29 December 1940 - Night of Heaviest Bombing
- 21 May 1941 - Final Raid of the Blitz

Key Figures

- King George VI
- Queen Elizabeth
- Hugh Dowding
- Sir Winston Churchill
- Adolf Hitler
- Hermann Goring

London on the Front Line

In the dying days of the summer of 1940, Hitler was desperate to launch his invasion of Britain. The Luftwaffe had failed to gain mastery of the skies over the English Channel during the summer-long Battle of Britain, so he changed tack. Instead of sending fighter planes against the Royal Air Force, he sent bombers to target civilians. Their first port of call was London.

London was a natural target. Not only was it the seat of government, the home of the Royal Family and heavily populated, but the Port of London was one of the busiest in the world. The city was also within easy range of the German bombers and the River Thames provided an easily recognisable route to the heart of the city.

Although the Blitz began in September 1940, London had been bombed before during World War I. The Blitz was new in that it was sustained, strategic bombing. The initial raids were during daylight. Late in the afternoon of 7 September 1940, the skies above London darkened as a swarm of almost 350 bombers, escorted by around 600 fighter planes, flew above the city. The planes got to London with little resistance as the RAF was taken by surprise at the change of tactics. Previously, the Luftwaffe had sought out RAF airfields and radar stations, so they were not prepared for an attack on London.

Once above the capital, the bombers released their loads, mainly over the docks of East London. Their assault began at 4.00 pm and lasted until 6.00 pm. Then, guided by the fires set by the first raid, a second wave of bombers arrived, unleashing an attack that lasted into the early hours of the next morning. At 4.30 am, when the Luftwaffe turned for home, it had destroyed more than 100,000 tons of shipping and killed more than 400 people, injuring more than 1,000 others.

Any hopes that the dreadful raid was an isolated incident were dashed on 8 September when the roar of the Luftwaffe's engines were heard again. In another daytime raid, 400 more Londoners lost their lives and more than 700 were injured. The bombers continued to return, bombing London for a total of 57 consecutive days.

A week into their campaign, on 15 September, the Germans launched two huge daylight raids on London. The objective was two-fold: Destroy the docks and railway, and force the RAF out to defend them. The Luftwaffe were confident that they would inflict great damage on the RAF's fighter planes and finally gain the air superiority that Hitler needed to launch Operation Sea Lion, his invasion of Britain. German intelligence suggested that the RAF was on the verge of collapse, a belief strengthened by the absence of any major defense of London in the first week of attacks. In fact, the RAF mounted a counter-attack and destroyed nearly one-fifth of the Luftwaffe's fighter planes on what would become known as Battle of Britain Day. Hitler accepted that he would not achieve air superiority over the RAF and shelved Operation Sea Lion. However, he did not lose faith in his Blitz strategy, still hoping that he could bomb the British public into capitulation.

Civilians shelter in Aldwych Station

Raids now switched, in the main, to nighttime. This was not only to increase panic in London, but to afford some protection of darkness to the bombers. Night defenses in London were inadequate. Searchlights did not have the power to reach high enough to light up bombers at high altitudes and there were not enough anti-aircraft guns. Although the number of anti-aircraft guns was increased, it was the improvement of the RAF's ability to fight at night, due to on-board radar, that proved successful in defending London.

On the ground, civilians did their best to go about their lives as normal despite the growing devastation around them. At night, people took shelter from the bombs. The government had encouraged people to build shelters in their backyards, but many either did not have these Anderson shelters, or did not like using them. Some people sheltered under their stairs, others sought out communal shelters. There were not enough purposely built deep communal shelters so Londoners took to the Tube stations. Initially, the government had resisted opening the stations, fearing that people would stay below ground after the end of a raid rather than go to work. There were also concerns that large groups of people would be open to anti-war propaganda. Both fears proved to be unfounded and indeed not only did business carry on, but people in the Tube stations found a positive and supportive community spirit. It was noticed that civilians were less likely to suffer shell shock and mental illness than their military counterparts. The government had set up clinics to help with an expected rush of shell shock cases, but these were closed down due to a lack of demand.

London's nightlife carried on during the Blitz.

Smoke rising from fires in Surrey docks

Theatres, cinemas, restaurants and pubs remained open and people visited them despite blackout conditions, doing their best to carry on as normal. At the Windmill Theatre, the cast and stage crew put on performances throughout the war, retreating below ground only when the bombing became very severe. The Theatre used the motto "We Never Closed" for many years.

While the working class found camaraderie in the Underground shelters, they found inspiration above ground in the form of the Royal Family. King George VI, Queen Elizabeth, and the Princesses Elizabeth and Margaret stayed in London for the duration of the war. The Queen declared that the children would only leave if she did and she would not leave unless the King did, and there was no possibility that he would ever go. The two princesses were sent to the relative safety of Windsor Castle, but the King and Queen remained in residence at Buckingham Palace.

Knowing that the King was at Buckingham Palace, the Luftwaffe targeted the Royal residence repeatedly. The Palace took 16 hits during the Blitz,

of which nine were direct. Fortunately, no one was seriously injured and there was little damage. The Queen felt a curious relief after the first bomb hit, remarking that she could now "look the East End in the face". She and the King did look the people of the East End, and the rest of London and the country, in the face, touring bombed areas and speaking to the survivors. The presence of the Royal family in the capital and out on the streets reassured the country and cemented the Royal family, and Princess Elizabeth (later Queen) in particular, into the public's affections.

Like the King and Queen, Winston Churchill remained in residence in the capital throughout the war. The Cabinet had a large underground bunker under government offices near Parliament Square from where they directed the war. Dormitories and bedrooms were provided for staff, but Churchill usually chose to sleep above ground. The BBC had radio equipment installed in the bunker, allowing Churchill to broadcast several speeches from the Cabinet War Rooms. His rousing words, urging the British to hold fast against Hitler, were an

A street of ruined houses in London

Barrage Balloons Over London

inspiration to the public and his presence at bomb sites was reassuring.

After nine months of relentless bombing, the Blitz came to an end. More than a million homes had been lost in London, along with 19 churches. Amazingly, St Paul's Cathedral emerged unscathed, though 16 of Wren's churches did not. In the City, 31 of the 34 ancient guildhalls were destroyed. Major institutions like the Bank of England and the Stock Exchange were spared. The human toll reached 40,000 dead and well more than125,000 injured.

For all the death and destruction, Hitler's campaign failed. Industry and transportation was dented, but not destroyed. Londoners were bloodied, but not broken and rather than breaking the nation's morale, Hitler unleashed a courageous and resilient spirit that passed into the common memory: the Blitz spirit.

Legacy

The Blitz, and the spirit of cheerfulness, camaraderie, and defiance that it fostered, passed into British mythology and are still referenced with pride today. The Royal Family and Winston Churchill reached new heights of popularity for staying in London with the people, and their place in the British public's affection still remains strong.

Sites to Visit

The Churchill War Rooms is the bunker where Winston Churchill sheltered during the Blitz. Preserved and under the auspices of the Imperial War Museum, the complex is open to the public.

Hermitage Memorial Park in Wapping has a commemorative sculpture in memory of civilian casualties of the Blitz. It is erected over the site of a communal bomb shelter.

The National Firefighters Memorial on the Jubilee Walkway commemorates the City's firefighters.

There are companies, like Blitzwalkers, who offer guided tours around the bombed areas of London.

Aldwych Tube Station was used as a shelter and is occasionally open for tours (see opening feature).

Films and DVD

Director John Boorman's fictionalized account of his childhood in the London Blitz paints an enchanting world of excitement and terror in "Hope and Glory "(1987). Available on DVD.

"Mrs Henderson Presents" (2006) is a warm and witty comedy set in the Windmill Theatre during the Blitz. Judi Dench and Bob Hoskins star.

"The Battle of Britain" is a classic film that focuses on the pilots who fought to protect London from German bombers.

Further Research

Philip Zielger uses his own experiences, as well as interviews, diaries and letters, to great effect in the excellent *London at War* (2002).

Poignant and funny, the people of the East End tell their own story of the Blitz in The War on our *Doorstep: London's East End and how the Blitz Changed it Forever* (2012)   Harriet Salisbury and the Museum of London

LOST IN THE POND

THE SEVEN-YEAR ITCH: A BRIT WHO'S BEEN AWAY TOO LONG
By Laurence Brown

In 1955, Marilyn Monroe delivered what has become one of the most iconic scenes in cinematic folklore. It was the one where her white dress billows upward against the gust of the New York City subway. That image has come to define Marilyn Monroe, but what is less known is the film to which it belongs.

It is called "The Seven Year Itch"—a film not primarily concerned, in fact, with Marilyn's character, but rather that of actor Tom Ewell. Ewell portrays Richard Sherman, a character that—after seven years—is beginning to question his marriage.

Today, in 2016, I can relate to Sherman's dilemma. You see, seven years ago I embarked on a relationship of my own. Not with another person, you understand, but with a little country known as the United States of America.

You could say it was one of those romantic fairy tales. After a rocky, recession-hit start to our courtship, America and I soon became inseparable—a little like Elizabeth Taylor and Richard Burton during their first marriage. The nation's citizenry warmed to me in a manner that suggested I was the "good" boyfriend, even if their reasoning was simply that I possessed a charming accent.

It seems funny looking back, but—for my part—I was in love with the United States. It treated me like no country had ever treated me and entertained me in a manner not altogether dissimilar to a screwball comedy from the 1980s: completely silly, but ultimately worthwhile. More than anything, from its rolling Kentucky hills to the otherworldly terrain of the Rocky Mountains, it was one of the most beautiful countries I had ever known.

Notice I said "one of," this will be important later on.

You see, it was alongside America that I truly discovered who I was—beginning my career as a writer and penning works for BBC America in the process. Moreover, I got myself into shape despite America's best efforts to prevent this. I also grew in confidence, spurred on—no doubt—by America's optimism and its reach-for-the-stars mentality.

Things were great. Things were magical. Things were almost exactly as they were in the movies.

And then something happened. Something quite unexpected. America started acting a little... strange.

At the risk of letting this column devolve into political drivel, let's just say that the 2016 Presidential Election happened. America showed, and continues to show, an ugly side of which I was previously unaware. Suddenly I didn't—as an immigrant—feel quite as at home as I once did, even if this hardline vitriol wasn't particularly geared toward British ex-pats. Nonetheless, every ounce of trust I had developed in America was steadfastly falling apart.

But to sound off like this makes it seem like it was all America's fault. It wasn't. I'd love to claim that America's sudden turn toward electoral lunacy and reality TV politics drove a wedge between us. I'd love to say that I was completely absolved of all guilt. The truth is, I was just as culpable. You see, a couple of years before the first candidate had even thrown his name into the hat, I was already sowing the seeds of our downfall.

This is because, just as Richard Sherman chose to exacerbate his itch by flirting with Marilyn Monroe, I exacerbated my own by dwelling on Great Britain. A lot.

Remember earlier when I told you that America was "one of" the most beautiful countries I had ever known? Well in relationship terms, there was one country with which America could not compete.

Britain—or more specifically, England—was all I'd ever known for 27 years of my life. You don't easily forget that. You don't suddenly sweep more than a quarter century of memories, feelings, and experiences under the rug. And even if you do, just a word or two here and there can bring them right back.

Increasingly, my written works for Lost in the Pond, BBC America, and Anglotopia brought me closer to not just a British readership, but a dedicated group of American Anglophiles, whose enthusiasm for all things British was certainly hard to resist. Before long, my interest in the country I'd left behind evolved into an obsession.

It was innocent at first—just the occasional glance at a red phone box or an annual viewing of "Love Actually". But then it escalated into something more serious. I started writing top fives on British destinations, filling my house with Union Jack paraphernalia, and devouring "Call the Midwife" and "Doctor Who" as if they were going out of style.

Actually, on the subject of "Doctor Who", I adapted my wardrobe—subconsciously at first—to be more reminiscent of our fabled time lord, splurging on the Tenth Doctor's tie, the Eleventh Doctor's fez (I assure you I only wear it at fancy dress parties), and the Twelfth Doctor's coat. I drew the line, however, at dressing like Jenny from "Call the Midwife". I couldn't get a uniform in my size.

The dialogue of these shows made me miss British words again and I fought like never before to retain my accent. I even took up tea towel collecting.

Actually, my collection consisted of more than just tea towels. After discovering Jungle Jim's International Store in Ohio and various shops specializing in British items, I bought virtually anything I could get my hands on. To this day, my kitchen is adorned of a tea pot, Bobby-on-the-beat egg cup holders, and a London-themed apron.

And so, no. Our downfall was just as much my fault as America's. I wanted something more. I wanted British weather in my life. I wanted British people, British homes, and British buses. I wanted British food, British money, and British scenery. I wanted… British iconography.

After all, what could be more iconic—subways and white dresses notwithstanding—than a red London bus, or a post office box, or the green hills of the English countryside? It's one thing to see them in an admittedly lovely magazine such as this, but to experience them up close is to know you have arrived in the most beautiful country in the world.

And so it's time for me to be honest with you, America. We've had brilliant times—no one can deny that. But after seven years, I am feeling the itch and you—despite your affinity for glitz and glamour—are not my Marilyn Monroe. Britain is. And I've been away too long.

Laurence is a British writer and humorist who lives in the United States. He also hosts the popular web series, Lost in the Pond on YouTube. He has an infuriating habit of taking America to task by pointing out how things are done in the UK. He really needs to stop this behavio(u)r. It's anti-American.

© Zed Martinez

10 BRITISH THINGS DOCTOR WHO EXPLAINED

By John Rabon

As a British cultural institution, "Doctor Who" certainly makes a lot of cultural references that might go over the heads of Americans. Whether foods, sweets, persons, current events, films, or other television programmes, "Doctor Who" often grounded itself in the real world by alluding to popular culture. Here's a list of a few things Doctor Who has brought to American attention.

Jelly Babies

A jelly candy covered in starch and similar to gummy bears, though different in consistency, this famous British sweet rose to prominence in "Doctor Who" courtesy of Tom Baker's Fourth Doctor. Clearly something picked up from the Doctor's time on Earth, the Fourth Doctor began offering them to anyone he met, whether friend or foe, to the point where "Would you like a Jelly Baby?" became something of his catchphrase. The sweets have appeared in other incarnations as well, such as when the Eighth Doctor offers them to a police officer or the twelfth Doctor does the same on the Orient Express.

Children's Programmes

Most notably, The Clangers and Teletubbies have appeared on the programme, which is interesting, considering that "Doctor Who" itself was intended as a children's programme to teach science and history. "The Clangers" was a programme about mice-like aliens who lived on the moon and spoke in a language that sounded like slide whistles. Roger Delgado's Master was fascinated by them in the story "The Sea Devils". In a nod to that episode, Jon Simm's Master was equally fascinated by the Teletubbies having televisions in their stomachs.

Bassett's

Bassett's is a major confectionery producer in the United Kingdom, making such favourite sweets as Liquorice Allsorts, Lemon Drops, and Jelly Babies. Since 1926, the company's mascot has been Bertie Basset, an anthropomorphic collection of the allsorts sweets. While not exactly a direct reference, villainous torturer Kandy Man, a robot made from candy, bore a strong enough resemblance to Bertie that Bassett's complained, launching a BBC investigation that ultimately revealed the connection to be entirely coincidental.

Scottish Independence

Between the failed independence vote in 2014 and the rise of the Scottish National Party in last year's elections, Scottish nationalism is enjoying more popularity than it has in centuries. This movement hasn't been lost on the writers of "Doctor Who" either. In "The Beast Below" when Amy Pond asks where the Scottish people are on the star whale, she's told that they wanted their own ship. A less-obvious reference was also made in "Deep Breath", where the newly-regenerated Twelfth Doctor (played with a Scottish accent by Scottish actor Peter Capaldi) comments on his very pronounced eyebrows by suggesting that they're independently cross and trying to secede from his face.

Tea

That quintessentially British drink (originally from Asia), multiple references have been made across the programme's history. From the Fifth Doctor's description of it in "The Awakening" to its ability to help stabilise the Tenth Doctor's regeneration, tea has been as much a part of "Doctor Who" as it is in the daily lives of most British people.

EastEnders

A soap opera based in the fictional East End London suburb of Walford, the programme's first encounter with Doctor Who occurred in the, perhaps, ill-conceived special "Dimensions in Time", in which several of the Doctor's enemies threatened Walford, requiring the Third, Fourth, Fifth, Sixth, and Seventh Doctors, along with their companions, to fight them off. While the story was never referred to again on either programme, the current version of Doctor Who has made several references to "EastEnders". The Tenth Doctor declared that one of the unluckiest sentences one could utter was "This is going to be the best Christmas Walford has ever had." During "Army of Ghosts" one of the Cybermen "ghosts" is shown to appear in the Queen Victoria Pub from the soap, causing disgruntled proprietress Peggy Mitchell to believe it's the ghost of "Dirty" Den Watts and ordering him out of her pub and she had done many times before to various characters.

Jammie Dodgers

This biscuit consisting of two shortbread wafers with a jelly filling seems to be a particular favourite of the

Eleventh Doctor. He attempts to fool the Daleks into believing one is a self-destruct button in "Victory of the Daleks". Later on, he asks for them in "The Impossible Astronaut" and "Night Terrors". He even took some off of Clara Oswald during their first meeting in the "The Bells of St. John".

Monty Python

One of Britain's greatest and most influential comedy programmes, most Americans are more familiar with the films than they are the sketches, if at all. While not a direct reference to Monty Python's Flying Circus, one of its key players, John Cleese, made a cameo appearance in the Fourth Doctor serial "City of Death" admiring the TARDIS as a work of art before the Doctor, Romana, and Duggan dematerialised in it. In the current programme, Missy uttered the classic line "Bring out your dead" when calling forth her Cyberarmy made the bodies of Earth's deceased.

Fish Fingers

Most Americans probably scratched their heads over what "fish fingers" were until they realised that the Doctor was talking about fish sticks. Unlike the Doctor, however, most Americans and Britons wouldn't combine them with custard as he did. I suppose we can chalk that up to the oddities of regeneration. The rest of us will stick with tartar sauce.

Reality Television

British reality programmes really got their moment to shine in "Bad Wolf/The Parting of the Ways" during the Ninth Doctor era. While some programmes were familiar to Americans including "Big Brother "and "The Weakest Link", fewer may have been aware of the British version of "What Not to Wear" with hosts Trinny Goodall and Susannah Constantine, who voiced robots in their image and stripped down Captain Jack Harkness, much like their real-life counterparts. The American version, of course, involved quite a lot less nudity. Other British reality and game shows referenced in the episode included Stars in their Eyes, Call My Bluff, Countdown, Ground Force, and Wipeout.

NAMES OF BRITAIN

The Various Names of Britain, Its Neighbours and Its Inhabitants

By Jonathan Thomas

There are so many names for the United Kingdom that it can be hard to keep them straight. Some were used interchangeably as if they mean the same thing. Some are used incorrectly. Oftentimes people are mistaken when they refer to something in Scotland as being in England or that the word 'English' means the same thing as 'British.'

So, we thought it would be fun to put together a list of words and explanations for some of the places and peoples in the United Kingdom.

UK - The official name is the United Kingdom of Great Britain and Northern Ireland, which consists of England, Wales, Scotland, and Northern Ireland.

(Great) Britain - The island of Great Britain itself but often used when talking about the United Kingdom. Does not include Northern Ireland.

British - A term usually used to mean anyone from the United Kingdom though this may annoy the Northern Irish. It is also not advisable to call a Scotsmen British. While they are technically British, they are Scottish first. Someone like Andy Murray is Scottish until he's winning at Wimbledon at which point he becomes British.

Britannia - An outdated Latin term for the island of Great Britain that was coined by the Romans. They also founded Londinium, the city that became London. Britannia is also the female symbol of the UK - the shield maiden used on older currency. Britannia was also a symbol of British Imperialism.

Briton - Essentially citizens of the United Kingdom, the Isle of Man, the Channel Islands, or of one of the British Overseas Territories. The shortened version is 'Brit' which is commonly used by Americans to refer to the British. There are many who don't like usage of that term.

The British Isles - Geographic name for the islands that make of Great Britain and Ireland, though it's falling out of use because the Irish don't like being called British.

Hibernia - Classical Latin name for Ireland.

Éire - Irish Gaelic for Ireland

Albion - Another outdated term for the island of Great Britain. This is the oldest known name of the island and comes from Ancient Greek.

Caledonia - The Latin name given to the northern part of Britannia which is now called Scotland.

Cymru - The Welsh language name for Wales.

Ulster - The northern, UK part of the island of Ireland (the independent Republic of Ireland is the bottom part).

England - The largest country in the United Kingdom, where most people live in the UK. South of Scotland and East of Wales.

English - 1. The language spoken by the British (but as in Scotland and Wales not the only language). 2. The people who live in England. Someone from Scotland is not English. Someone from Wales is not English. Only someone from England is English

Blighty - An older term for 'Britain' that evokes misty-eyed golden images of Britain. 'Dear Old Blighty.'

Rosbif - A derogatory French term used by the French to describe the British. Because the British love Roast Beef.

Sassenach - Term used by the Scottish and other Celts to describe the English.

Team GB - The official Olympics team for Scotland, England, Wales and Northern Ireland. Some people believe the name discriminates against the Northern Irish.

Grande Bretagne - French for Great Britain.

Angleterre - French for England.

Grossbritannien - German for Great Britain

Gran Bretagna - Italian for Great Britain

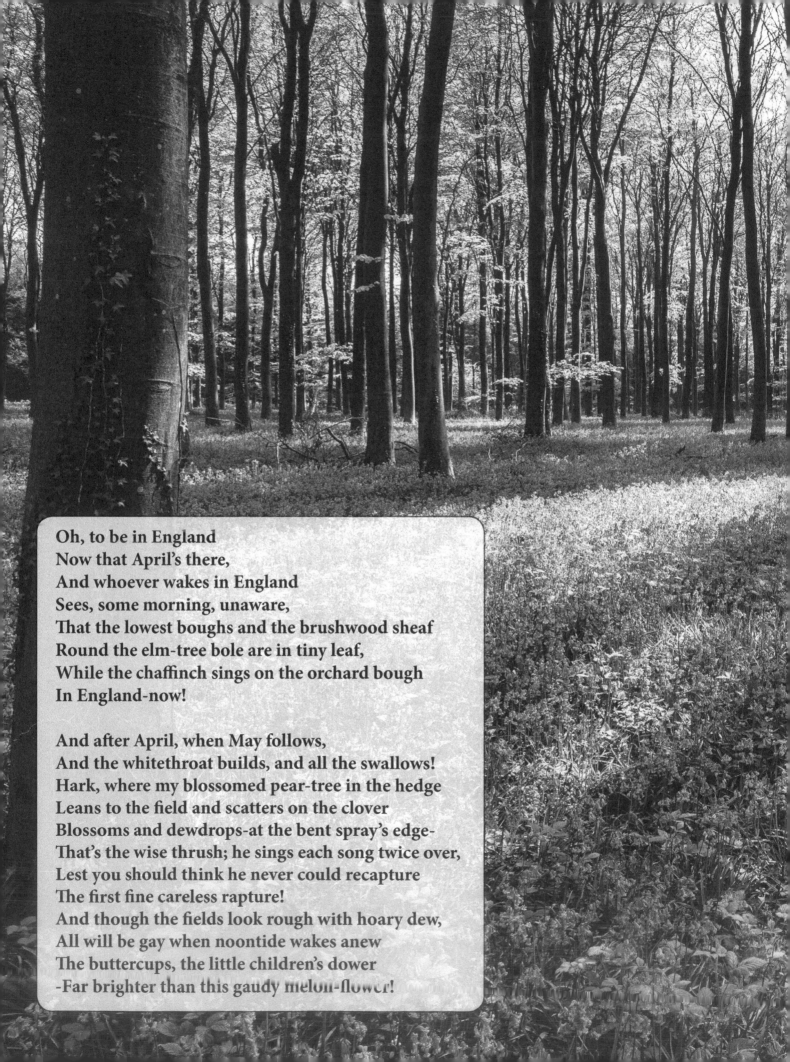

Oh, to be in England
Now that April's there,
And whoever wakes in England
Sees, some morning, unaware,
That the lowest boughs and the brushwood sheaf
Round the elm-tree bole are in tiny leaf,
While the chaffinch sings on the orchard bough
In England-now!

And after April, when May follows,
And the whitethroat builds, and all the swallows!
Hark, where my blossomed pear-tree in the hedge
Leans to the field and scatters on the clover
Blossoms and dewdrops-at the bent spray's edge-
That's the wise thrush; he sings each song twice over,
Lest you should think he never could recapture
The first fine careless rapture!
And though the fields look rough with hoary dew,
All will be gay when noontide wakes anew
The buttercups, the little children's dower
-Far brighter than this gaudy melon-flower!

Home Thoughts, From Abroad
By Robert Browning

Bluebells in Wepham Woods © phil_bird

GREAT BRITISH BUILDINGS
Canterbury Cathedral
By John Rabon

© NigelSpiers

The home of the Church of England and, in many ways, Britain's spiritual centre. Since almost the very introduction of Christianity to Britain, Canterbury has had an important role in the nation's relationship with the Church. In 596, Pope Gregory the Great sent a Benedictine monk named Augustine as a missionary to the Anglo-Saxons. Setting himself up in Canterbury at St. Martin's (which remains the oldest church still in use), he would begin work on the first cathedral in 597, eventually being ordained as the first Archbishop of Canterbury by Gregory. This house of worship was completed in 602.

The Saxons would expand upon Augustine of Canterbury's cathedral for the next 400 years, but sadly, all their work would be destroyed by a fire that claimed the original cathedral in 1067. King William I, who had appointed Bishop Lanfranc as the new Archbishop in 1070, began work on a replacement at the same site. The base of Augustine's cathedral would form the foundation of Lanfranc's. Lanfranc had previous experience in church construction, having rebuilt the abbey

church of St. Etienne in Caen when he was abbot there.

It took another seven years for Lanfranc's cathedral to take shape and it was consecrated in 1077. He constructed the cathedral as a cruciform building with a nave that had nine bays, two towers on the west end, aisle-less transepts with apsidal chapels, a low crossing tower, and a choir with three apses. On the exterior, the cathedral's steeple was topped with a golden statue of an angel. His successor, Archbishop Anselm, with the direction of Prior Ernulf, had the eastern transept demolished and extended it out another 198 feet, adding two more chapels in the process that became known as St. Anselm's Chapel and St. Andrew's Chapel. The choir was expanded so much that it practically made up a chapel unto itself and with the completion by Ernulf's successor Conrad in 1126, an elaborate crypt was also constructed that remains today.

In the meantime, Canterbury Cathedral became a major pilgrimage destination, as depicted in Geoffrey Chaucer's *The Canterbury Tales*. This only increased after the martyrdom of Thomas a Becket

by King Henry II's knights in 1170. The knights, who allegedly mistakenly believed that Henry had ordered Becket's death, carried it out in the North-West Transept, which is now known as the Martyrdom. Four years later, another fire destroyed the eastern expansion in 1174 and the choir was rebuilt out even further into what we know as Trinity Chapel, which includes a shrine to Becket above the spot where his body lies in the crypt. Burial near Becket's shrine was considered to be especially holy and King Henry IV and Edward, the Black Prince, were buried near to him.

The nave was then rebuilt in the 14th century and by the 15th, Lanfranc's original tower was torn down and the "Bell Harry" Tower was constructed to replace it, with the great bell ("Harry") in that tower was not added until the 17th century. Prior to this, Canterbury was not spared the dissolution of the monasteries and surrendered to King Henry VIII in 1539. The cathedral was later damaged during the reign of Oliver Cromwell, whose men raided many of the cathedral's artefacts to make it more fitting of the Puritan attitude towards church decoration.

One of the last major works of construction

was the demolition of the North-West Tower from Lanfranc's original Norman design to a tower that mirrored its South-West counterpart. Begun in the 1830s, this was part of the renovations done during the Victorian era that also included the Trinity Chapel roof that had been destroyed by a fire in 1874. Today, as it has for centuries, Canterbury Cathedral stands out from nearly every vantage point in the city and serves as a major place of worship for millions of people with more than 2,000 services held there every year.

The cathedral is open daily to visitors, times vary based on the time of year but generally 9 am to 5 pm. It opens for visitors later on Sunday after noon so people can worship in peace. There are 3 guided tours a day at 10.30, 12.00 and 2.00 pm. There is an admission charge of £12 (about $18) for adults and £8 (about $12) for children. You can save a few pounds by booking ahead on their website.

If you come to worship, it's of course free to come into the church but keep in mind you're not really allowed to wander around. There is evensong nightly which is also free to attend. See their website for precise timings: http://www.canterbury-cathedral.org/

ANGLOPHILE 101
WEIGHTS & MEASURES

Britain is a hybrid country. It invented the system of Imperial measurements but they now mostly use the metric system. The key word there is mostly. As with all things British, it's more complicated but no worries, we're going to try and break it down for you.

Temperature

Britain uses the metric system for temperature measurement in all situations. For those not familiar, it's really simple but 0 degrees is freezing and 100 degrees is boiling. But where it gets confusing is when you're trying to read the weather forecast. Having to convert is a bunch of math that most people don't want to do. So, here's a quick breakdown of what those temperatures mean (with a little humor thrown in).

-10 Siberia
-5 Freezing your Bollocks Off
0 Cold
5 Do I Need a Coat?
10 Basically a Spring Day
15 Heatwave
20 Pleasant
25 A Real Heatwave (And you start to realize that AirCon isn't common in Britain)
30 Basically Dubai
35 Typical Southern USA Summer
40 The Face of the Sun

Weight

Now weights and measures are another matter. Officially Britain uses the metric system; in practice there are still a few holdouts.

The metric system is based on 10. For length:

10 millimeters (mm) = 1 centimeter (cm)
10 centimeters = 1 decimeter (dm) = 100 millimeters
100 centimeter = 1 meter (m) = 1,000 millimeters

1000 meters = 1 kilometer (km)

While this is the official system, in practice, speed is still measured in Imperial Miles, speedometers are in miles, but you buy gas by the litre. It's so odd really. Roads signs will all be written in miles as well.

Here is a breakdown for weight:

10 milligrams (mg) = 1 centigram (cg)
10 centigrams = 1 decigram (dg) = 100 milligrams
10 decigrams = 1 gram (g) = 1,000 milligrams
10 grams = 1 dekagram (dag)
10 dekagrams = 1 hectogram (hg) = 100 grams
10 hectograms = 1 kilogram (kg) = 1,000 grams
1,000 kilograms = 1 metric ton (t)

In practice you will mostly see weights broken down by grams or kilograms. However, there is a completely different weight the British used called 'Stone.' This is usually used when measuring the weight of a person. A stone is equal to 14 lbs or 6.3503 kilograms. A person would say they weigh 6 stone and that would translate to 84 lbs. It's an odd system.

Volume

Here is a breakdown for volume:

10 milliliters (ml) = 1 centiliter (cl)
10 centiliters = 1 deciliter (dl) = 100 milliliters
10 deciliters = 1 liter (l) = 1,000 milliliters
10 liters = 1 dekaliter (dal)
10 dekaliters = 1 hectoliter (hl) = 100 liters
10 hectoliters = 1 kiloliter (kl) = 1,000 liters

In practice you'll generally see liquids in milliliters, liters or kiloliters. Beer and Milk are the only things sold by the pint nowadays. FYI, a British pint is 20 fluid ounces compared to an American pint which is 16 fluid ounces.

Great British Art - The Fighting Temeraire
by JMW Turner

JMW Turner is probably Britain's most favorite landscape printer. Turner had a particularly great skill at painting the sky at sunset and that is what provides the beautiful light for The Fighting Termeraire. This painting is a tribute to the famous fighting ship from the Battle of Trafalgar. This scene symbolises the passing of the age of sail to the age of steam - the old girl is being towed by a steam powered boat to the shipbreakers. It's a scene he personally witnessed. It was recently voted Britain's favorite painting of all time (beating Constable's Hay Wain which was featured last month). This painting is on display with many other famous Turner paintings at the National Gallery in London.

GREAT BRITISH ICONS
The Routemaster Bus
By David Goodfellow

The Routemaster bus ran throughout London for the second half of the 20th century. It became the standard bus instantly recognised by everyone and eventually exported around the world. The design incorporated several features new on buses, such as a lightweight aluminium body, power-steering, an automatic gearbox and power-braking. The 'hop on, hop off' design allowed for rapid use of the bus outside designated stops and was a large factor in its enduring popularity, despite the safety risk. Although production ceased in the 1960s, the bus survived the privatisation of London Transport and was even re-furbished to extend its life. The last bus was taken out of service in 2005, although a heritage route still allows visitors to ride this classic bus.

In 1829, inspired by a similar service he had seen in Paris, George Shillibeer began a horse-drawn 'omnibus' service in London. The first route was from Paddington station to the Bank of England at a fare of one shilling. Since this is almost £40 today, the stop at the bank was probably necessary. He borrowed the name for his service from the French too, which became contracted to 'bus' quite quickly. Other similar services followed, and in 1855 a joint Anglo-French company, Compagnie Generale des

Key Facts

- Greatly loved symbol of London life
- Ran from 1956 to 2005
- Iconic red double-decker featured in many films
- Innovative early use of aluminum technology developed during WWII

Omnibus de Londres, soon to become the London General Omnibus Company, bought out almost all the services and formed a monopoly. By the early 20th century, the company was operating a mixed fleet of horse-drawn and motorised buses and in 1912 LGOC was bought out by the operators of the London Underground and the joint business soon became known as London Transport.

The earliest motorizsed buses were modeled on the horse-drawn omnibus, with an open upper deck reached by an outside staircase, with the driver seated in an open compartment at the front. Already the buses were painted red, having earlier been decorated with the Union Jack.

© Victor Keech

The Old and The New

The most famous early bus was the B-type, nicknamed 'Ole Bill', which was even used as a troop-carrier during WWI. This bus, usually considered the first mass-produced commercial vehicle, was designed by LGCO's chief motor engineer, Frank Searle, and assembled at a factory in Blackhorse Lane, Walthamstow. After the amalgamation with the Underground service, the manufacturing section of the company became the Associated Equipment Company, usually simply know as ACE. Besides making buses, ACE also built lorries, initially based on the bus chassis. In 1927, AEC moved its manufacturing from Walthamstow to a new factory in Southall, Middlesex.

Frank Searle was replaced by G. J. Rackham, who had worked for the American firm, Yellow Coach, during the 1920s. ACE built a wide range of buses, both single and double-decker, for London Transport and for many parts of the Empire. The first double-decker with a roof appeared in the 1920s with a six-wheel luxury vehicle running from Cricklewood to Grosvenor Place. By the 1930s, buses in a style that would become familiar began

to appear on the streets of London, notable the AEC Regent III RT, which entered service in 1938 and continued until 1954, with several thousand being manufactured during that period. This bus had enclosed decks and a large rear platform with enclosed steps to the upper level. The driver sat in a separate compartment at the front, and a conductor sold tickets and directed passengers.

As the economic recovery from WWII took hold, the need for a new bus became apparent. The tram service, which also ran in London, had been replaced by trolley-buses and these now were removed from the streets, as car traffic grew, and were replaced by bus routes. A new, more fuel-efficient bus was needed that was cheaper to service and carried more passengers. Between 1947-1956, a team directed by A.A.M. Durrant and Colin Curtis designed the Routemaster bus for ACE, which came out three-quarters of a ton lighter than the old RT models, and carried 64 seated passengers against the 56 of the older buses. The styling of the bus was by Douglas Scott and did not deviate greatly from the RT style, retaining the open rear deck and

Unique Rear Entry with Conductor

Routemasters on Show

separated driver compartment. Seen from the front the Routemaster had a broader radiator than the narrow design of the RT buses. The bus was built with the new war-time material, aluminium, and also features novel innovations like independent front suspension, power steering, a fully automatic gearbox and hydraulic power braking.

The open rear deck was hugely popular with passengers, since it allowed anyone to board the bus when stationary, or even slow-moving, away from the designated stops. For this reason, this style is often called a 'hop on, hop off' bus. Despite its popularity, this feature became a factor in its withdrawal, since mounting and leaving a moving bus caused around 12 fatalities a year.

The Routemaster bus became the iconic London bus during the post-war period. Between its arrival on the streets on the 8 February 1956 and the production of the last bus in1968, 2,647 basic model Routemasters were built, with another 200 single-decker coaches and some experimental front-entrance versions also being built during that time. The bus began to be withdrawn from service in

September 1982, chiefly because London Transport moved to single-driver buses, eliminating the conductor, to cut costs. By 1988, the Routemaster was largely confined to inner-city routes, but continued through the privatisation of the service which began in 1989.

Although no longer being produced, and with the ACE plants now closed, the buses were still structurally sound and it made economic sense for the new private firms to keep them on the roads. So a process of restoration began, with buses being refurbished and even in the new millennium London Transport, now controlled by the socialist mayor Ken Livingstone, started buying back and refurbishing buses that had earlier been sold to other companies, in the UK and overseas.

However, pressure to replace the bus, for safety reasons and to provide handicapped transport, continued and the last bus on a standard route (route 159) ran on 9 December 2005. The bus entered the Brixton depot just after 2 o'clock in the afternoon, having been delayed by the huge crowds that had gathered and who completely blocked the

Routemaster Interior

road. A much loved icon of London was retired but the idea behind the Routemaster endures in its modern replacement the New Routemaster.

Sites to Visit and Further Research

There is a Heritage Routemaster bus route 15 between Trafalgar Square and the Tower of London, via St Paul's Cathedral. Buses run 09.30 to 6.30 every day (except Christmas Day).

The London Bus Museum is part of the Brooklands Museum, on Brooklands Road, Weybridge. The museum is open every day except for the Christmas period, from 10 am to 5 pm in summer, and till 4 pm in winter. The museum has a large range of vintage buses, set against backdrops of street-life of the various periods.

There is a biography of the bus, *The Bus We Loved: London's Affair with the Routemaster*, by Travis Elborough. User manuals and repair manuals are also available.

The New Routemaster

BRIT BOOK CORNER

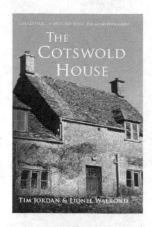

The Cotswold House

This new architectural book from Amberley will interest those who are curious about the architecture of the beautiful Cotswolds area of England. The history behind the very recognizable Cotswold stone homes is fascinating and goes back hundreds of years. This book attempts to break down the different styles, the different construction methods and the different layouts that make up the vernacular of the Cotswolds. It will interest those with a fascination with architectural history on a local scale, it will not really interest the casual Cotswold visitor. But if you're curious to learn more about what's behind the stones, then this book is for you. It's filled with hundreds of beautiful pictures of houses in the Cotswolds, worth the price of admission itself! SRP: $34.95

Winston Churchill Reporting - Adventures of a Young War Correspondent

Another year, another book about Churchill. While there are ample books that focus on his young life (and there's even an excellent movie) - *Winston Churchill Reporting* focuses on the phase of Churchill's life where he made a name for himself as a journalist and war correspondent. Simon Read writes excellently about the various adventures that Churchill went on as he developed two careers in parallel - one in the British Army and one as a writer on the side. Read does an excellent job of placing Churchill within the late-Victorian British Empire era. We tend to only think of Churchill in the context of World War II so it's easy to forget that he's a product of the Empire. The book is an excellent narrative of his life - pulling in resources from third parties and not just Churchill's own writings (he also wrote extensively about this part of his life). I didn't think there was much new ground to cover but there is a lot here and makes it worth reading for any Churchillian. The book starts with his adventures in Cuba during its war of Independence from Spain followed by adventures in Afghanistan and the Sudan. A good bulk of the book is dedicated to his time in South Africa during the Second Boer War. There are elements missing, while Read does a great job of building up the background info for the conflicts - he also kind of leaves the reader hanging as to what happened after. After Churchill leaves Cuba, so does the writing and we don't know how the war turned out - same with the Boer War section - instead of telling us how the Boer war ended - we got a short summary of Churchill's life afterwards when his career really took off. Churchill comes alive as a character in his own story - though not having been raised in the bloody late-Victorian era, it's really hard to sympathize with his imperial bloodlust and medal chasing. Still, it's an interesting insight into a young man on the move who had grand plans. The book also glosses over whether or not the Britain's imperial ambitions and slaughter of natives was a good or bad thing - that debate is for other books. Well worth a read for fans of Churchill. SRP: $26.99

Local Eats London By Natasha McGuinness

This is a bit of an odd book. It's a guidebook to food in London without being a guidebook at all. The concept behind the book is to show you the typical meals you should look for in London if you're traveling there. It's not concerned with the places you should actually eat at but rather the different foods that are typically British and what to expect from them. As a seasoned London traveler familiar with British food and the various options, it wasn't very useful for me. Still, if you're not familiar with British cuisine it's a good starter guide to the types of food you can expect on your next trip. The illustrations by Danielle Kroll are colourful and add a lot of character to the book. SRP: $14.99

HENRICVS, VII

HENRY VII
THE FIRST TUDOR KING

Henry VII secured his right to the throne of England at the famous Battle of Bosworth Field (1485) where his army defeated that of King Richard III and killed him. Henry ended the Wars of the Roses and began the great dynasty of the House of Tudor, stabilising a country scarred by years of civil war and political upheaval and uniting Europe, at least for a time. When he wasn't fighting rebel forces intent on ousting him from the throne, Henry spent his time collecting revenue in ways that were revealed after his death to have been less than legal, but it was a full treasury he left behind on his death in 1509.

Henry VII's questionable claim to the English throne came about by chance, when King Richard II decided to legitimise Henry's great-grandmother and her siblings.

Richard II's uncle, John of Gaunt was in a long relationship with a lady called Katherine Swynford, despite the fact that he was married to another woman. Together John and Katherine had four children who were, by law, bastards born out of wedlock and not entitled to claim any inheritance or titles from John.

Richard was in a constant state of political warfare with his uncles, including John of Gaunt, and feared John's legitimate son, Henry, Earl of Derby, was plotting to take his throne (which he later did and became King Henry IV). So, to satisfy his uncle and block Derby from the throne, Richard II had John and Katherine's four children, the Beauforts as they later became known, legitimised.

Henry VII's grandmother was the widow of Henry V, Catherine of Valois, and Sir Owen Tudor, a former gentleman usher at Queen Catherine's court. Catherine and Owen's first child, Edmund Tudor, was Henry VII's father and half-brother of King Henry VI. As half-brother to the King, Edmund was made the Earl of Richmond. Edmund married Lady Margaret Beaufort, the King's cousin and a great-grand-daughter of John of Gaunt and Katherine Swynford. Edmund was captured while fighting for

Richard III

Henry VI in South Wales against the Yorkists and died while 13 year-old Margaret was pregnant with Henry.

Born and raised a Welshman, Henry never set foot outside of Wales until he was 14 years old. Following the Battle of Tewkesbury that saw his fellow Lancastrians all but wiped out, Henry was sent to live in France in exile. By 1483, Henry's mother was promoting him in powerful circles as the next king, an alternative to Richard III. On Christmas Day 1483, Henry pledged to marry Elizabeth of York, King Edward IV's eldest daughter and heir.

With the support of his mother, wife and the King of France, Henry was confident of his entitlement to the throne and began to raise an army to invade England. Richard III attempted to have him extradited from Brittany but Henry escaped to France where he was greeted with a gift of French troops. Henry landed in Pembrokeshire in 1485 and marched towards England with an army of 5,000 soldiers. Richard III's army significantly outnumbered that of Henry but during the famous Battle of Bosworth Field on 22 August 1485, many of Richard's key allies switched sides or simply left the battlefield. Richard III was killed, effectively ending the War of the Roses and making Henry VII the next king.

Battle of Bosworth Field by Philip James de Loutherbourg

King Henry VII's coronation took place at Westminster Abbey on 30 October 1485. To help solidify his position as the rightful king not only by conquest but also by inheritance, Henry honoured his pledge to marry Elizabeth of York. The wedding took place at Westminster on 18 January 1486, successfully united the warring houses of York and Lancaster and gave any children of Henry and Elizabeth a strong claim to the throne.

Henry took all of the precautions he could think of against potential revolts and usurpers to his throne. He had 10-year-old Edward, Earl of Warwick arrested and taken to the Tower of London for fear that he may have a rival claim to his throne. But despite his best efforts, the early years of Henry's reign were troubled by rebellions. In 1486, the rebellion of the Stafford brothers and Viscount Lovell threatened Henry's throne.

In 1487, Yorkist troops led by a boy, Lambert Simnel, who claimed to be the Earl of Warwick invaded England and in 1490, a man, Perkin Warbeck, claiming to be Richard, one of the 'Princes in the Tower' invaded Ireland in 1491 and later England in 1495 with the support of James IV of Scotland. In an attempt to protect himself, Henry founded the 'Yeoman of the Guard' on 22 August

1485, a personal bodyguard that still exists and is the oldest British military corps in existence.

When he wasn't fighting rebellions and executing anyone with even the most tenuous

Elizabeth of York

The Tudor Rose

connection to his throne, Henry VII was examining the royal accounts. Henry tightened royal administration and perfected his own ruthless system for collecting revenue resulting in a £1.5 million surplus in the national accounts by the time he died. Henry cared little for the interference of Parliament and summoned it seven times for a total of 25 weeks over his entire reign of 24 years.

Henry and his wife Elizabeth had seven children together and rather than adopting the costly and aggressive strategy of invasion and war favoured by some of his predecessors, Henry used dynastic royal marriages to make alliances in Europe and establish the Tudor dynasty in England. Henry and Elizabeth's daughter, Margaret, was married to James IV of Scotland, Mary was married to Louis XII, King of France and Arthur Tudor married Catherine of Aragon. When Arthur died suddenly in 1502, Henry VII sought an arranged a papal dispensation from Pope Julius II that gave permission for his younger son Henry, who would go on to become Henry VIII, to marry Catherine, his brother's widow. This dispensation would later go on to play a key role in Henry VIII's separation of the Church of England from the Roman Catholic Church.

Queen Elizabeth died on 11 February 1503 from infection, a result of childbirth on 2 February 1503 and Henry is thought to have been overcome by grief. Immediately following Elizabeth's death Henry became gravely ill and almost died himself. Although he made vague plans to remarry and have more children, Henry was alone for the remainder of his life and died of tuberculosis at Richmond Palace on 21April 1509, tended to by his mother who followed him to the grave two months later.

Legacy Today

Henry VII is credited with ending the War of the Roses and founding the great and powerful Tudor dynasty. Despite spending the majority of his reign defending his shaky claim to the English throne through brutal and extreme measures, Henry was also able to strengthen the English government and rebuild the royal finance. Although he won his throne through battle, like the sovereign powers of Louis XI of France and Ferdinand II of Aragon, Henry's approach to statecraft was multi-faceted and forward thinking. By marrying his children into powerful royal families in the likes of Scotland and Aragon, Henry increased England's influence in Europe and secured the closest thing to peace in the middle ages.

Film & TV

- "The White Queen" (2013) TV series
- "Henry VIII"(2003) TV Series
- "Looking for Richard" (1996)
- "Richard III" (1995)
- "Shadow of the Tower" (1972) TV series
- "An Age of Kings" (1960) TV series
- "Richard III" (1955)
- "Richard III" (1912) silent film

Further Research

- Weir, Alison (2008) *Henry VIII: King and Court*
- Bacon, Francis and Thompson, Brian (2007) *the History of the Reign of King Henry VII*
- Cunningham, Sean (2007) Henry VII
- Chrimes, S.B. (1999) *Henry VII the English Monarch Series*
- Penn, Thomas (2011) *Winter King: Henry VII and the Dawn of Tudor England*

Locations to Visit

- Henry VII was born in Pembroke Castle in Wales.
- Bosworth Battle Heritage Centre is located in Leicestershire, United Kingdom.
- Henry VII frequented the medieval Eltham Palace. Henry VIII and his siblings were raised there.
- He died at Richmond Palace which no longer exists, but was buried at Westminster Abbey.

TOASTING TOLKIEN & LEWIS

A Day in Oxford

By Jonathan Thomas

We all have places where we've been for a brief snippets of time and hope that we can one day go back. For me, that place is Oxford, England. I've dreamed of its spires for many years and while I was never able to be a student there, I've held a reverence and respect for the place. We visited once in 2012, it was a flying visit and we didn't have the chance to explore, the hotel on the outskirts was a stop on the way to somewhere else and we were jet lagged. Our major memory was driving a crying baby around the Oxford Ring Road at 2 in the morning. Oxford deserved more from us than that and I've dreamed of going back since.

As we planned our recent trip to London, I was determined to spend one day outside of London. It's something we always encourage visitors to London to do - there's so much more to see and do in England than all the wonders that London has to offer. Even if you can get away for a day - you can see something amazing and unexpected. It did not take long for me to decide that my day trip would be spent in Oxford. I bought a recent guidebook to the city and began planning.

As most of our trip would be spent in London, we would not have a rental car (hire car in British speak) this time around so getting there would require a trip on the train. As a train enthusiast, I was thrilled about the prospect. I was able to book advance tickets from the US using the official rail booking website and managed two return tickets to Oxford for £52 (about $75). Trains run practically every 15 minutes from London Paddington directly to Oxford. There is another option to get to Oxford that is much cheaper, the Oxford Tube, it's a bus service running every 10 minutes 24/7 from London Victoria (tickets start at £18 return - about $25). I like trains so we opted for the train.

Paddington Station is probably my most favorite station in London and that's not just because of it's association with a certain bear. It's simply a beautiful building. We arrived about 45 minutes before our train and marveled at the stunning Victorian architecture. The station was alive with the buzz of London morning commuters. A voice on the intercom reads out platforms and destinations. Paddington always has this feeling of griminess and history - in a good way. I was both happy and dismayed to see that the station is in the middle of refurbishment. Much of the beautiful architecture was obscured by plastic and scaffolding but I was glad to see the building get some restoration attention. We quickly found our train, hopped on board and found our reserved seats (we recommend always reserving a seat - on busy trains you're not necessarily guaranteed a seat unless you reserve one).

Our train departed on time and sped its way into the outer London suburbs very quickly. As it was the end of February, we had a lovely overcast day but that still didn't make the countryside any less beautiful as it passed by. I'm always surprised at how fast trains move in England - if you've ever ridden the train in the USA, you know how slow it can be. Our train arrived at Didcot and we had to change trains (this was part of our ticket, it made it cheaper). We found our next platform and waited for the train, we didn't have to wait long. We settled in our seats and about 15 minutes later we arrived at Oxford's railway station.

Compared to London Paddington, Oxford's station is nothing to write home about. It's basically a modern shed with no character - not quite the welcome you're expecting coming into a historic city like Oxford. The station is close to the city center so you have to walk a bit to get to where all the 'Oxford action' is. We arrived at about 10am so the city was buzzing with students on their way to classes and visitors coming to see the city. It was a treat to watch Oxford wake up for the day. Broad Street is sort of considered central Oxford's main area so we follow that map we brought along to get to it. It's a main shopping street and there is access to many of the universities and museums from the roads leading off it.

Our first goal for the day was to go on an Oxford Walking Tour. When you arrive to the main area of Broad Street you'll be bombarded with options for tours, bus rides and whatnot. There are plenty of options there but we planned in advance to take a tour with the conveniently named Oxford Walking Tours (http://www.oxfordwalkingtours.com/), a company that's been around for more than 35 years and operates the 'official' tours of Oxford and its many colleges. We arrived just in time for the 11 am tour - which was very good as they only do the tour with four or more people and we brought the count up to four. The price of the tour is £9.95 and includes admission to the colleges (some tours don't include admission - watch out for this!). Tour times vary based on the time of year but they're generally

Broad Street

every hour. You can book in advance online but there's really no need to - it won't save you any money.

Oxford University is a strange and unique place. It operates as its own little world under its own rules and doesn't take kindly to anybody dictating what they should and should not do. The rules are arcane, strange and somewhat incomprehensible to outsiders. It's best not to think of Oxford University as one place but rather a grouping of 38 separate colleges that all kind of work together. Each college is different, has its own history, its own rules and way of doing things. Annoyingly for visitors they have different policies on outside visitors which make it difficult to plan a day poking around. This is understandable, during term time (when classes are in session), Oxford is an industry town - students are hard at work with their studies and tourists poking around every nook and cranny would be disruptive. Even more strangely, while the colleges manage the individual tutorials of students, the university handles lectures, exams, labs and the libraries. You can think of the individual colleges

as more like a private club of fellow students. There is even an Oxford College that has no students and is 'fellows' only - All Souls College. You'll find that many of the traditions that we follow for universities and graduation ceremonies have their origins here at Oxford (the robes for example).

Our tour guide spent a lot of time filling us in on the secretive world of Oxford and it was all fascinating stuff though admittedly it was difficult to take it all in at once. The tour started on time and it was just four of us, so it was a nice and intimate tour. The college we toured was Balliol College (pronounced Bailey-Ole). Balliol is one of the oldest colleges in the university and along with Merton and University College, considered one of the founding colleges (they all argue amongst themselves who was the first). Amongst the college's most famous alumni are three former prime ministers; H. H. Asquith, Harold Macmillan and Edward Heath), five Nobel laureates and a number of literary figures and philosophers. Political economist Adam Smith, who wrote the *Wealth of Nations* and basically created the modern concepts of capitalism, is perhaps the best

Balliol Quad

Bailliol Coat of Arms

Dining Hall at Balliol

Altar in Balliol's Church

known alumnus of the college. When you tour the college greens and buildings, you get the impression that yes, this is the place that people who go on to run the world we live in fit in well.

Student life at Oxford is much different than it is as school here in the USA. First of all, you don't really go to classes. Yes, there are important lectures (which are managed by the university but not your college) but your education is largely self-guided under the management of a Tutor (the titular Oxford Don). You form a personal relationship with your Tutor and they usher you through the archaic Oxford system (and you better be on good terms as you are stuck with them for your whole school career). You will spend most of your time buried in books, researching in Oxford's cavernous libraries and are expected to write several 2,000 word or more research papers a week. You will then experience a grilling from your Tutor on the content of your papers and expected to defend points and research you've used. It can be an awful experience. But it's a system that's worked for hundreds of years. And then there are the final exams, handled at the

university level. Life will vary greatly based on the college you attend - no Oxford experience will be the same.

The tour took us through the grounds of Balliol - we started with exploring the various courtyards and then we were able to go into the main dining hall which was like a scene from Harry Potter (it's no coincidence that the film versions of the books were filmed in Oxford and took inspiration from its medieval architecture). The most amazing aspect about the dining hall is not its beautiful vaulted ceiling but rather the fact the there is a full table service at every meal - while our guide took us around, they were in the middle of setting the tables for the lunch service. It is all proper ship shape and Bristol fashion the cutlery and plates are immaculate (all with the school's crest). Compared to the cafeteria where I spent my school lunches in college, it was quite a sight to see and made me rather envious.

After the visit to the dining hall, we explored the school's own church which was a beautiful structure. Outside Balliol, we went on to explore the city of

Sheldonian Theatre

Bodleian Library

Scriptum Stationary Store

Oxford itself. The guide was very knowledgeable and knew what each building's function was. While this was a walking tour, it does not exert you, there's probably a mile of actual walking and more standing as you listen to the guide explain various things. Our next stop was the Sheldonian theatre, a beautiful half circle theatre that you've probably seen many times if you're a fan of Inspector Morse. The building was designed by a certain Sir Christopher Wren, whom you may know as the architect of St Paul's Cathedral in London. The Sheldonian is certainly a stately looking building and is a great example of neo-Palladian architecture. The theatre is still used today for plays, concerts, lectures and University ceremonies (like graduations). The guide said that it was usually really easy to get a good last minute deal on a concert or play so always plan ahead and see if you can take in a show when you're there.

Next we took in the Bodleian Library, which is probably the very definition of what a library should be. Unfortunately, the library is not open to visitors as it's a working library, but the chamber below is open to the public and features some beautiful Gothic architecture along with several artifacts from the university's history. Outside the Bodleian is a courtyard that is also the center of academic life where exams were often performed - you can see the doors to the various department exam rooms. Above the courtyard sits a room that was also where Charles I held Parliament while he was holed up in Oxford during the English Civil Wars (Oxford was a staunchly Royalist town). It's safe to say that Oxford is dripping in history, when something has been around for more than 800 years, it's certainly hard not to be.

The guide was also a fount of local knowledge on what we should see and do with the rest of our visit to the city - his advice was helpful. He also had a lot of information on the other colleges that were open on that day to visit. We were pressed for time so opted to leave Balliol as our Oxford College experience but I think we'll be back on a future trip to explore some of the other colleges. It was with great dismay that we learned that the day we visited, a Monday, was the day that many Museums in Oxford are actually closed. Oxford is home to some world class museums like the Ashmolean and Pitt-Rivers Museum, unfortunately they were closed the day we visited, which was a shame as we wanted to see them. But that just gives us more reasons

Top Tips for a Day in Oxford

- **Frequent trains from London Paddington Railway Station.**
- **Oxford Tube is cheap and run every 10 minutes from London Victoria**
- **Arrive early to make the most of the day**
- **Take a walking tour, we recommend Oxford Walking Tours**
- **Go to Blackwell's Bookshop - basically book heaven.**
- **Museums in Oxford are usually closed on Mondays. Check ahead!**
- **The Oxford Guidebook from Let's Go was useful in our planning.**
- **Climb St Mary's Tower for great views of the city (but not if you're claustrophobic).**
- **Tour at least one college.**
- **For a hearty lunch try Brown's Cafe in the Covered Market**
- **Plenty of shopping on Broad Street and on the High Street.**

to come back again. Despite the museums being closed, there was still much we wanted to see.

After our tour, we were quite peckish for lunch. So headed towards the Oxford Covered Market on the advice of our tour guide. But on our way we stopped at a store that Mrs Anglotopia read about in our guidebook. Scriptum is a hard store to describe. They advertise themselves a stationery store, and they have that in spades - fancy pens, beautiful blank journals but they also have books, mini statues, and other types of ephemera that you would expect to find in a store in Oxford, England. The best way to describe it would be it felt like a store in Diagon Alley in Harry Potter. If you want a lovely keepsake that you'll likely only to find in Oxford, I would recommend a stop here. I opted for some very expensive fancy bookmarks than came in a pack of 10 that would go nicely in my library back home.

After we lightened our wallets at Scriptum, we headed for the Oxford Covered Market. The market dates back to 1774 and has been in operation pretty much every day since then. And like all wonderful things in England, it's under threat as the council is trying to raise the rents on businesses that have had

Oxford Covered Market

their homes in the market for generations. We opted for lunch at Brown Cafe, which has been there since 1924. It was a simple cafe that served classic British fare. Mrs Anglotopia had bangers & mash for lunch while I had chicken and chips.

The food was simple, affordable, (lunch was £13 for two people) and delicious. We highly recommend this place for lunch. It's a small place and can be a bit cramped. The crowd is a mixture of tourists looking for a good lunch and students catching a quick meal outside their college on their way to classes. It's all very romantic. Makes me wish I was a student again, this time at Oxford. We nosed around the market and enjoyed browsing the various merchants and supporting an important local institution. If you don't want a hot lunch, there are plenty of food vendors where you can buy fresh food and put together a picnic. We hope that the vendors can fight back and keep this treasure of place alive for future generations.

After a lovely lunch, we headed out of the market for Oxford High Street, which is a nice thoroughfare

of lovely shops and important attractions to see. One of the places I had to stop in was the Oxford University Press official bookshop which is exactly what it says on the tin and I couldn't help but pick up a few books that caught my interest (though ironically neither had anything to do with Britain - one was about Napoleon and the other was about astronomy). We also wanted to pop into the official Oxford University Gift Shop. Mrs Anglotopia and I watch the Oxford-Cambridge Boat Races every year and with them coming up, we wanted to pick up official Crew shirts. Unfortunately the staff didn't have them in stock yet and they were generally unhelpful towards us which put us off buying anything else (as did the high prices). We found perfectly nice Crew gear at an unofficial Oxford shop down the street (with much better prices).

Oxford High Street still suffers from the disease afflicting most High Streets in the UK - a proliferation of chain stores and restaurants. Still, there's plenty of unique shops you can't find anywhere else. I was chuffed to see an outpost of Ede

St Mary's Church

Climbing down the St Mary's Tower

All Souls College

One of the Views from St Mary's Church Tower

& Ravenscroft, which is London's oldest tailor and the establishment that often provides ceremonial robes to Britain's Lords and Ladies (and Kings and Queens). It was founded in 1689, long before the Unites States of America was even an idea.

Across from the shopping is St Mary's Church. St Mary's is the 'official' church of Oxford University and the University grew up around it. It's a beautiful old building but its most famous aspect is its spire - one of the most beautiful in England. The church is open daily to visitors but the star attraction is the spire - if you pay a small fee in the gift shop (£4 or about $6) you can climb to the top of the tower. We highly recommend doing this. The views from the tower in all four directions are stunning - you can see the whole city and its medieval street layout before you. We were lucky in that the sun came out in time for our climb so the whole city had a golden hue. It was perfection. Now, I'm not generally a claustrophobic person but as I climbed the tower in a winter coat and backpack, I began to feel pretty anxious as there is only room for one person to

climb at a time in any direction. Once you begin you have no choice but to keep going up and there are A LOT of stairs. So, if you're intimidated by very tight spaces, you may want to avoid this. Still, if you can handle it, it's worth the climb for the views alone (and it's not so bad going down). The church also has a lovely cafe with ample teas and treats (along with a loo if you're caught short after sightseeing all day).

After the tower climb we walked down the high street and explored the various shops and businesses that Oxford had to offer. It's very much a city that people live in - it's not just a tourist destination. Broad Street is very much the heart of Oxford and we loved exploring the shops. But as we neared the end of our day, it was time for something I had been greatly looking forward to. A visit to Blackwell's Bookshop.

For those that don't know, Blackwell's is quite possibly the best bookshop in the world. I'd never been and quite a few of my Anglophile friends told me to be sure I stopped in. And wow. What an

The Basement at Blackwell's Books

amazing place. It doesn't look big from the outside - it just takes up two small shopfronts. But once you go inside, you've stepped into a TARDIS. The bookshop is massive. I had no idea the scale of the place. I followed the stairs to the basement and was presented with a wide open expanse that was the biggest number of books I'd ever seen in one place. When I was done filling my hands with books there, I climbed the stairs back to the top, thinking I was done. That's when I found another staircase leading up and discovered there are actually four more floors, filled with books.

It was heaven.

I found so many books I needed a basket to carry them all. I found books on British history, culture and travel - books I would not be able to find back home in the USA. I found myself ticking off half my Amazon UK wishlist. And best of all they had a 3 for 2 offer on where you buy three books in the same category, you get one for free. I abused this offer greatly. Let it be said that I showed considerable restraint on my first visit to Blackwell's. I'd found so many books I began to worry about how I was going to get them home - we'd only brought one big piece of luggage with us and all the books were not going

to fit in it. Thankfully Blackwell's have a solution for that. For a small fee (proportional to the cost of the books) they will ship your books home for you. Their staff were very helpful and made sure to sign me up for their customer rewards program. They packed up my books and they arrived at home about a week later to be placed into my eager library. I will definitely be going back to book heaven on our next trip to England. I think a stop at Blackwell's will become a new tradition for us.

Speaking of books, Oxford obviously has a rich literary heritage as many great British writers were students or professors there. The most famous grouping were the Inklings, who met in the 1930s and 40s and discussed literary issues of the day. Its two most famous members were JRR Tolkien and CS Lewis who were good friends and would later be literary titans. They would have regular meetings in The Eagle and Child pub, right across the street from the main university buildings. I'm happy to report that this pub still exists and has become a bit of attraction itself and many make their own literary pilgrimages to the place. So, as a Tolkien fan, I had to have a meal there where literary greats used to drink their pints.

Where Tolkien and Lewis drak their pints

Adult Courses at Oxford

It is actually possible to study at Oxford as a 'mature' student. Berkeley out of California offers summer programs at Oxford for interested mature students or enthusiasts. You go over for 3 weeks, study a particular subject, you get to stay in a college and get the full Oxford experience (including a grilling from a Tutor). Graduate level credit is awarded to successful passing. There are field trips related to your course and more. It's sounds like a dream for anyone who was unable to attend Oxford as an undergraduate. The program is not cheap - almost $7,000 (and that doesn't include airfare) but it's certainly on my 'Britain Bucket List.' The course line-up changes every years so be sure to check their website for more info at: http://extension.berkeley.edu/static/oxford/

The pub is full of typical character though it's a lot less smoky than it would have been back in the Inkling's days (smoking was banned in pubs a few years ago). The pub has many different artifacts from their famous patrons, who used to meet in the Rabbit Room near the front. Sadly, when we arrived some other fellow literary fans were already occupying the space, so we had to sit elsewhere. Still, we ordered a meal and toasted to Tolkien and Lewis. This is not really a bad thing, but the pub has been bought out by a pub chain. So, while it maintains its unique character and history, the food is pretty much the same as you'd find at any other pub owned by the chain. Don't get me wrong, the food was good but it was nothing special. It didn't matter though, we weren't there for the food.

If you want to learn more about the Inklings, Blackwell's has a whole section dedicated to them where you can read about the group, buy their various books and soak up the literary heritage. I can't wait to read more about them! I've personally never read CS Lewis but I think now is a good time to start. And perhaps a Tolkien re-read is on the horizon. I've always loved the *Lord of the Rings Trilogy* books along with the movies.

By this point in the day, we were exhausted (or cream crackered as the British say). We'd had a very hearty dinner at the Eagle and Child and since everything was beginning to close, our day in Oxford was coming to an end. The only problem was that we had train tickets booked for 8.30 pm. It was 5.45 and we were ready to head back to London. We did not have an open ticket and we didn't relish waiting in the station for almost three hours. We headed to the station, walking down quiet residential Oxford streets enjoying the ambiance of a lively college town. When we arrived at the station I explained our predicament to the ticket agent and he was able to issue us new tickets for a small fee and additional small fare - it was worth it to not wait. So, we caught an early train back to London in time to catch the evening Telly.

One day in Oxford was not enough. We certainly enjoyed dipping our toes into Oxford but we've discovered a place that we now love very much and will be returning to often. There are still the museums to visit that were closed and we'd like to explore more of the individual colleges. Not to mention visit Blackwell's again. We'll be back soon enough and we can't wait.

A WARM, DRY PLACE
THE CABMEN'S SHELTERS
By David Styles

L ondon is huge, and there are a great number of sites that will take your interest. When you traverse the capital from one popular tourist 'hot spot' to another I would urge you to take the advice of Samuel Johnson who once memorably gave these pearls of wisdom to his drinking partner Boswell:

"It is not in the showy evolutions of buildings, but in the multiplicity of human habitations which are crowded together, that the wonderful immensity of London consists."

One human habitation worth seeking out are the often overlooked Green Cabbie Huts that are a quaint anachronism from Victorian days and very, very English. These small shelters providing refreshments are dotted around London's streets, with many open to the public for takeaway sales, they are well worth a visit.

London cabs have been licensed since 1639, and by 1860 there were 4,600 plying for trade. Being out in all weathers poor health and conditions have historically dogged the trade, never more so than in those Victorian times.

At that time, the cab-driver's vehicle of choice was a Hansom Cab, a horse-drawn carriage which was open to the elements for the cabbie. He was expected to 'sit on the box' in rain, snow, cold and wind waiting for a fare and the only place of sustenance and comfort was a public house.

In January 1875, Captain Armstrong, ex-soldier and editor of *The Globe* newspaper based in Fleet Street who lived in north London's St. John's Wood, sent his manservant out into a raging blizzard to engage a taxi to take him to his office. The manservant eventually found the cabbies enjoying each other's company in a local hostelry, each displaying varying levels of intoxication.

Returning a full hour later and soaked to the skin, Captain Armstrong asked his man why he had been so long to be told that although there were cabs on the local rank all the cabmen were certainly in no condition to take him to Fleet Street.

Now at that time the Temperance Society was at the peak of its powers, and excessive intake of alcohol was frowned upon. So in line with the Victorian ethos of public service, Captain

© oyxman

Armstrong decided to do something about this and came up with the idea of dedicated shelters for cabbies' use next to the cab ranks.

With the assistance of the 73 year-old 7th Earl of Shaftesbury (Theatreland's Shaftesbury Avenue takes his name), and a few like-minded philanthropists, they founded the Cabmen's Shelter Fund which took up offices at 19 Buckingham Street, just off the Strand.

The aim was to build and run shelters at the busiest cab stands within a six-mile radius of Charing Cross considered to be the centre of London. Each shelter would have an attendant and provide 'good and wholesome refreshments at moderate prices'. This would both address the problems of food and shelter and, more importantly, reduce the cabbies' temptation to indulge in alcohol.

Many shelters had books and newspapers – donated by the benefactors and publishers – for cabbies to read and provide up-to-date topics of conversation. Publications included such riveting reads as: *The Graphic, Aunt Judy's Magazine, Fun and The Animal World.*

Gambling, swearing, and political discussion was strictly forbidden – the last condition was almost certainly ignored as it would be today.

The Prince of Wales – later to become King Edward VII, put in a few bob. Duke of Westminster provided Piccadilly's shelter, but who was Mrs Braithwaite, the benefactor behind the one in Hobart's Place? Or Miss Roget, who financed the Knightsbridge Shelter?

One shelter erected in Old Palace Yard, Westminster, was paid for by members of both Houses of Parliament, presumably to ensure the politicians would never have to wait for a cab to get them home after a hard day debating in the Chamber.

The first of the early shelters was opened in 1875 in Acacia Avenue, St. John's Wood (handily for Captain Armstrong who happened to live nearby) by Arthur Kinnaird MP before a crowd of 100.

Between 1875-1950, 47 of these shelters were built at a cost of £200 each. At first the shelters had no provision for supplying meals, but by 1882 larger shelters were erected, which included a small kitchen so that hot meals and drinks could be provided by the shelter-keeper, or for a charge of half-a-penny the attendant would cook any food brought in by a cabbie.

By now the watermen (many now out of work due to the new bridges crossing the Thames) seem to have become the London cab stand officials who ensured that the cab horses had enough water to drink. Originally, the watermen seem to have been hangers-on who fetched buckets of water from the nearest pump, or did other services for hackney coachmen and their passengers in exchange for tips. By 1850, the waterman had become a quasi-police official charged not only with supplying water, but also with keeping order on the stands and administering punishments after disturbances. Ironically, the watermen were paid by the cab drivers themselves from a compulsory fee of one penny for each time they came onto the stand, and a further half penny each time they were hired while resting in the shelter. By 1860, watermen had been absorbed into the police force and were not only paid a regular wage of fifteen shillings a week, but were also issued with uniforms.

Only a dozen or so Cabbies' Green Shelters remain. They're worth searching out, because their appearance – a cross between a cricket pavilion and a large garden shed – serves to underscore the truth that the cab trade is so ancient that it pre-existed the modern city.

The proviso laid down by the Metropolitan Police that, as these shelters were situated on the public highway, they could be no larger than a horse and cart. This has given them their characteristic style.

They are of rectangular shape with dimensions described as '7 bays long, by 3 bays wide'. Windows are situated on the upper part of the walls in the middle bay of the short sides, and in the second, fourth and sixth bay on the long sides, with the middle window replaced by a door at one end.

The roof was originally felt-clad, but is now more often protected from the elements by traditional slates or oak roof shingles and pitched. In the middle of each shelter was a wood burning stove with a flue leading up a single vent in the roof to carry off the smoke, this square slatted ventilation structure on the roof is not dissimilar to a dovecote. There are railings around the shelters that were intended for the tethering of the Hansom cab's horses. Some of these railings can still be seen today.

The upper panels between the windows are decorated with a pattern of holes that include a monogram CSF, standing for Cabmen Shelter Fund, which most shelters have. However, some shelters have either glass or wood in the top panels instead. The whole shelter is always painted the distinctive Dulux Buckingham Paradise 1 Green.

The shelters really are tiny with enough space for only 10-13 diners. Two benches run along the white walls behind two long, thin Formica tables with hinged leaves for squeezing into your place. Two people can pass with care in the central aisle, if they turn sideways. At the far end the shelter the proprietor resplendent in their apron moves between a cooker, fridge and packed shelves of sliced bread and chutney.

The shelters seem to take on the characteristics of the areas that they reside. The Sloane Street Shelter has a awning sponsored by top real estate agent Winkworth protecting customers from the sun. The shelter gleams like a designer emporium with seasonal hanging baskets reflecting perhaps the nearby Chelsea Flower Show organised nearby. The Kensington Gardens trees overhanging the All Nations have left the roof rustically bowed and mossy. While in St. John's Wood, a stone's throw from Regents Park, is surrounded by exotic potted plants.

Many cabbie huts were destroyed in the Blitz and with the subsequent post-war redevelopment and road widening the shelters went into decline leaving only 13. When the Greater London Council folded, the baton was passed to the Heritage of London Trust, which has underwritten the renovation of all but two of the shelters, at a cost of £25,000 each. They are now Grade II listed buildings and protected by English Heritage. On 27 September 1966, The Cabmen's Shelter Fund was registered with the Charity Commission and the shelters are now run by tenants who pay a contribution to the Charity to maintain the shelters.

One shelter which stood at Hyde Park Corner

> 'Offsales are for all but only those with "The Knowledge" get a seat inside.'

© Justin Leighton / Alamy

until it was pulled down to make way for the Piccadilly Underpass was often frequented by polar explorer Sir Ernest Shackleton. The regulars, prior to his last expedition, presented him with a set of pipes and a pipe rack. He later died at sea but his letter thanking them hung on the shelter wall until the shelter's demolition.

While you explore London traditional food and drink, at very reasonable prices, may be purchased from the surviving shelters. Ask and you might be invited to look inside these quaint throwbacks from a bygone era.

Chelsea Embankment ('The Pier')

This shelter overlooking Albert Bridge has one of the most romantic locations for a greasy spoon. Nicknamed 'The Pier' due to its proximity to Cadogan Pier, it was, in the 1970s, also called 'The Kremlin' as it once had a clientele of left-wing cabbies. Alas it awaits a new tenant and remains unused.

Embankment Place

Non-cabbies are normally prohibited from entering, but sometimes they make an exception. Prince Charles once popped in for a chat with the cabbies at Hanover Square.

St. George's Church in Hanover Square has for many years given out small amounts of money to the homeless who sleep under the church's portico at night. As in many parts of London, the numbers of rough sleepers and other disadvantaged people has been increasing, and often this money is spent on alcohol or drugs, rather than on food and drink. The Vestry has now started to issue "refreshment coupons" valued at £2 each, which may be exchanged for food and drink at the shelter.

Kensington Park Road

Almost opposite the Albert Hall near to the site of the Great Exhibition of 1850 'All Nations' refers to the diversity of visitors visiting the famous Victorian spectacle.

Pont Street

This shelter spent most of its life in Leicester Square. When vehicles were banned in the late 1980s, the shelter became obsolete. The decision was soon taken to move the shelter to Russell Square. A plaque outside attests that this shelter was presented by Sir Squire Bancroft a famous actor/manager in 1901. Now the shelter has been relocated again, this time to a different part of Russell Square to make way for the 2012 Olympics.

St. George's Square

In the 1960s, developers knocked down four ancient streets running down to Temple Place to allow for a hotel to be built presumably for American tourists who hoped they could see just the sort of quaint roads they had destroyed. When the hotel reached completion the architects were amazed to find that just at the spot they'd planned to put their grand hotel entrance there was a green cabbie's shelter.

With typical corporate stupidity they tried to use their financial might to have the shelter removed by the authorities, but they were told that the shelter had been there since 1880 and was staying put. With the image of their rich guests being greeted by a ramshackle old shelter they were forced to beg for its removal. For a price the shelter was duly moved a few yards down the road away from the hotel's lobby.

The green shelter is still there, but the hotel has been demolished – awaiting redevelopment.

Thurloe Place ('The Bell and Horns')

Opposite the Victoria and Albert Museum, this shelter derives its nickname from a pub which once stood on the opposite side of the road. As you leave the museum's main entrance the shelter stands in the middle of the road.

Warwick Avenue

Surrounded by multi-million pound houses, this newly refurbished shelter is located in Little Venice close to the Grand Union Canal. The proprietor Pat Carter featured on the television programme "Ready, Steady, Cook" alongside celebrity cook Ainsley Harriott.

Wellington Place ('The Chapel')

This shelter is close to the famous Lord's Cricket ground and not far from the original erected by Captain Armstrong.

So when you visit London take Samuel Johnson's advice (he did after all write the first English dictionary) and seek out all those interesting nooks and crannies. There is more to London than waxworks and beefeaters.

A Licensed London Cab Driver for nearly 20 years, David Styles writes extensively about London. His work has been featured in many publications and posts twice weekly at CabbieBlog.com

THE SLANG PAGE
Translating British Speak - Best British Insults

No one knows quite how to insult like the British. They can make the most biting and cruel insults sounds like a compliment. After all, anything sounds better with a British accent. But it's also useful to know British insults because most Americans won't know what they mean, so you can use them on unsuspecting victims.

Here is our list of the 10 best British insults and their context and usage. In the examples we're going to pick on a bloke named George.

Lost the Plot - Someone who has lost their mind or their intelligence. "My God, George really has lost the plot, hasn't he?"

Barmy - Something stupid or crazy. "How did you think that was going to go, George? It was a barmy idea to begin with."

Gormless - Someone who completely lacks common sense. "George is my mate, but he really is gormless."

Manky - Something that is disgusting. "George, don't hand me that manky old towel from the laundry."

Pillock - An idiot. "George is such a pillock."

Plonker - An idiot. "George is such a plonker."

Knob Head - The knob is British slang for the end of the male genitalia. A knob head is, well, an idiot. "Don't be such a knob head, George."

Bell End - Means the same as Knob End. "George is such a bell end."

Lazy Sod - Useless idiot. Not only is the person an idiot, but they're lazy as well. "George, you're such a lazy sod."

Daft as a Brush - Someone who is silly or crazy. "George, you really are daft as a brush."

Not Batting on a Full Wicket - Someone who's rather eccentric or odd. "George really isn't batting on a full wicket, is he?"

Airy-fairy - Not strong, weak. "George is such an airy-fairy."

Mad as a bag of ferrets - Someone who is crazy. "George really is mad a bag of ferrets, isn't he?"

Pug-Ugly - A very ugly person. "George has a face only a mother could love, he's pug-ugly."

Piss Off - Go away. "George, how many times have I told you to piss off?"

Git - A special kind of moron. "George is such a git."

Prat - An incompetent, stupid, or foolish person; an idiot. "George, piss off you prat."

Nutter - Someone who's clearly lost their mind. "George is a nutter."

Chav - American equivalent would be white trash / lower class. "It doesn't get more chavvy than George, does it?"

Slag - A very derogatory and sexist term for a loose woman. "George is such a git he can only get with slags."

Twit - An idiot. "George, don't be such a Twit."

Ankle-biters - A not-so-nice term for children. "George can't stop having so many ankle-biters."

We've left out some of the worst ones because, well, they're not appropriate for a family magazine! After writing all those examples out, I'm really feeling sorry for George now. Let's go down the pub and buy him a pint to say sorry.